MY LITTLE BIRDIE TO A DIAGNOSIS

When Different Takes Flight

Erica L. Taylor

— MY LITTLE —
BIRDIE
TO A DIAGNOSIS

WHEN DIFFERENT TAKES FLIGHT

A MEMOIR OF STRUGGLE, ACCEPTANCE, AND
THE BEAUTIFUL JOURNEY OF RAISING
A CHILD WITH AUTISM

ERICA L. TAYLOR

My Little Birdie to a Diagnosis

Published 2025 by Taylormade Publishing

1st edition

"My Little Birdie to a Diagnosis" is a work of nonfiction. I have documented all events based on my memory, journals, and personal records. For legal reasons, I have intentionally omitted the names of individuals and specific locations. This book is not intended to harm anyone; instead, it aims to inspire others to speak up and trust their observations.

Paperback ISBN: 979-8-9987023-0-3
Hardcover ISBN: 979-8-9987023-1-0

For inquiries, please contact
Website: www.mylittlebirdie51509.com
mylittlebirdie51509@gmail.com
Instagram: @autismmom51509

Dedication

To My One and Only Son, Landon

Thank you for believing in yourself and placing your trust in me.

Acknowledgements

There are no words to express how grateful I am to those who understood my concerns and helped my son grow into the young man he is today. We could not have succeeded without you.

Thank you to all the physicians, nurses, therapists, teachers, aides, bus drivers, counselors, athletic coaches, and child study team members who helped my son attain his full potential. You did everything you could to ensure he received excellent care, support, and treatment, and you taught him how to speak up for himself in all areas of his life. I will never forget your patience, devotion, and determination to see my son flourish and celebrate his accomplishments. I genuinely appreciate your dedication, as you were all vital to my son's successful development. You have made a tremendous impact on all our lives, and we are forever grateful to you.

I would also like to thank my family and friends for their love, support, and belief in Landon. Your love and support have been a genuine source of strength for both of us. I am immensely grateful to everyone. We love you.

THANK YOU!

Different But Never Less

I am a person who is special, just like you,
With strengths and weaknesses, both tried and true.
I love to learn new things, but please take it slow,
your patience will help me, as together we grow.

I felt safe with an aid by my side in my younger days,
I thrived on structure, and routine paves my ways.
I dream of becoming a Chef, to cook and create,
to draw and to help others, oh, how I can't wait!

My thoughts may unfold in a different, cool style,
I treasure my family and respect every mile.
When life feels overwhelming, I seek coping skills,
Bowling became my sport, where I find joy and thrill.

Some noises can echo, too loud for my ears,
I've learned to cover them when anxiety nears.
Certain fabrics may pinch, though they seem like a tease,
and when I'm excited, I may flap with ease.

Meltdowns may linger, or vanish like dew,
I need time to process what's happening too.
Starting a conversation can feel like a climb,
I wonder if you're genuine or just passing time.

Social interactions can be tricky for me,
Past bullying shadows my need to be free.
I'd love to be friends, believe me, it's true,
But I may need guidance to help me break through.

Sometimes I misunderstand what you say,
show me with actions; let's learn through play.
I'm smart and I'm willing, though help can be key,
Finding shared interests can be hard for me.

If you see me alone, it's not that I choose,
Reaching out feels tough, yet I'd love to cruise.
I may have Autism, but I'm just like you,
Different in ways, yet never less than true.

So, let's share this journey, you and I side by side,
with kindness and patience, let friendship be our guide.

Preface

I've carried the profound yet unfinished story of my son within me for many years. My Little Birdie to a Diagnosis is more than a memoir; it's a journey of love, self-discovery, advocacy, hope, and resilience. It honors the beautiful spectrum of human differences, and the powerful lessons learned through acceptance and embracing what makes us unique.

This book is more than just storytelling it's a purpose-driven message. I write to inspire, to connect, and to offer comfort to families walking a similar path. From the struggles that shaped us to the moments that filled us with pride, each chapter reveals a part of our truth. Through our story, I hope to encourage others to embrace their own path, find strength in vulnerability, speak openly, seek support, and keep moving forward.

This memoir is a heartfelt conversation. My hope, dear reader, is that somewhere within these pages, you'll find reflections or moments that echo your own experience and that they offer you comfort, clarity, or courage. May this story invite you to live a life rooted in love, grounded in acceptance, rich in connection, and shaped by purpose. Most of all, may it remind you to celebrate your own voice, your own strength, and your own extraordinary individuality.

Tell me and I forget
Teach me and I remember
Involve me and I learn.

Benjamin Franklin

TABLE OF CONTENTS

Introduction

Embracing the Horizon

A Mother's Promise

The moment I found out I was pregnant, everything changed. It was a bright, bustling Friday morning when I saw that faint, unmistakable sign. Tucked away in the bathroom at work, the world seemed to pause as the reality washed over me —a tiny life had chosen me. Awe settled in, quickly joined by a jolt of nervous energy that coursed through my body. I sat silently in the bathroom stall staring at four positive pregnancy tests, my thoughts racing as I imagined the road ahead.

Just weeks earlier, my life was filled with ordinary distractions: work deadlines, late nights with friends, softball, and the carefree rhythm of being young and untethered. Never in my wildest dreams did I expect a single line on a test to change everything. But there I was, staring at it, overcome by a rush of emotions— joy, fear, and a depth of love I hadn't known was possible.

In that instant, I made a promise to myself. I would lead with love, patience, kindness, and strength. I would be the mother my child needed, protecting them at all costs. I pictured the late-night feedings, the first smiles, the first steps, the first words, and the day I would hold my baby for the very first time. I already knew—no moment would compare to that. I was ready to give everything: every sacrifice, every sleepless night, every ounce of love I had.

As the weeks passed and my belly grew, the reality of pregnancy became more tangible. The gentle and vigorous kicks, the steady weight gain, relentless hunger, and persistent cravings—all signified that my baby was developing well and thriving. My body changed, and with each shift, my bond with this tiny life deepened.

I whispered to my baby in quiet moments, sharing my hopes, my worries, and all the dreams I carried for both of us. Each day strengthened my understanding of motherhood, not just as a role— but as a transformation.

With that growing love came clarity. I began to grasp what so many had tried to explain but couldn't quite put into words: the enormity of a mother's love. It lived in the quickening of my heartbeat at the first flutter, in the way I instinctively placed my hand on my belly, reaching for connection that defied explanation. It was vast, consuming, and beautiful, filling me with excitement to learn the sex of my baby.

The day had arrived. It was a cool, beautiful October morning. The sun peeked through the golden leaves, casting a warm glow that seemed to dance upon the earth. I admired the landscape as my son's father drove, realizing that this day would turn my world around even more.

As I approached the hospital, a flutter of butterflies filled my stomach. Today was the day I would find out the gender of my baby—a moment I had waited for with eager anticipation. I had already chosen a girl's name, something lyrical and delicate, but the boy's name still eluded me. What truly mattered was my baby's health. Still, I harbored a secret wish tucked away in my heart; I longed for a little boy.

After checking in and registering, I felt an overwhelming rush of emotions. Excitement mixed with anxiety surged within. Every step toward the ultrasound room felt surreal. I could hardly believe that my pregnancy was becoming more real with each passing moment. *"Erica, please follow me,"* a technician called with a smile.

I grabbed my things and followed her down the corridor, the sterile scent of the hospital mixing with the sweetness of anticipation. The room was dimly lit, comfortable but clinical. Climbing up onto the table, a wave of impatience washed over me. I wanted to know, but I didn't want this moment to end too quickly.

With practiced ease, the technician glided the transducer across my belly. The screen flickered to life, revealing the shadowy forms of my baby. My heart raced, and I barely processed the technician's concentrated expression as I stared at the blurry images.

And then I heard it—the words that would forever change my life. *"It's a boy!"* she announced, her voice filled with joy. My heart soared, and suddenly, the world around me faded into the background as I soaked in the words. *"He's very active and healthy,"* she continued, and I leaned closer to the screen, my breath caught in my throat.

At that moment, time stood still. My dreams and hopes crystallized into a single image—a little boy, vibrant and full of life. I felt tears prick at my eyes, a rush of relief and happiness crashing over me like a wave. My secret wish had come true.

I spent what felt like hours examining the images on the screen, each flicker and movement representing the little soul that would soon be part of my life. As I lay there, I imagined the adventures we would have together, the bond we would share, the lessons we'd learn, and the joy filled with laughter and love.

When the ultrasound ended and I left the room, the weight of the world lifted from my shoulders. I felt empowered and hopeful, ready to face the journey ahead. I would cherish this boy—my son—beyond measure. As I walked out of the hospital, the cool October air wrapped around me like a warm embrace. I knew everything was about to change, and I couldn't wait for it to begin.

I imagined the moment I would meet him for the first time, my heart racing at the thought. I pictured his tiny fingers—delicate and soft—curling around my own. His little feet would be so small, each toe perfectly formed and barely the length of my thumb. I could almost see his button nose, slightly crinkled, and his wide, sparkling eyes, perhaps a deep shade of blue or brown. The air would be filled with that unmistakable scent of a baby—a sweet, powdery fragrance that wraps around you.

One evening, I sat in the corner in my son's nursery, hands resting on my belly, and felt the fullness of that connection. Soon, my son would enter the world, and life would never be the same. Each day brought a mix of strength and vulnerability, and I welcomed the coming storm of motherhood with open arms.

I was no longer just a young woman moving through life—I was being shaped into something new. Motherhood was calling me to grow in humility, resilience, and boundless love. I felt connected to every mother who came before me, united by a shared devotion that transcended time.

As the sun dipped below the horizon, casting soft light through the window, I felt calm. I was ready. Ready to guide, protect, and love this little life unconditionally. The road ahead would be far from easy, but I believed deeply and truly that it would be the most meaningful journey of my life.

Yet he still didn't have a name. For weeks, I had felt the weight of not having a name for my precious baby boy. I had cycled through countless names, scribbling them down in a notebook, only to cross them out one by one. Nothing seemed to fit, and I worried I would never find the perfect name.

One evening, my son's father and I were chatting about everything and nothing with my best friend and her then-boyfriend at a restaurant. As she shared her hopes and dreams of becoming a mother one day, she mentioned the names she had loved for a boy. That's when she said it: "*Landon.*"

The moment the name left her lips; I felt a connection. It was like a spark ignited within me. "*Landon,*" I whispered, letting it roll around in my mind and tasting its sweetness. I thought the name was perfect for my baby boy.

Just as she suggested, *"You should take the name 'Landon',"* my belly gave a powerful kick. Startled, I instinctively placed my hands over the spot where I had felt the movement. *"I think he likes Landon, too!"* I declared with a grin, and to my amazement, Landon kicked again, a confident little thump.

We all burst into laughter, the kind that bubbles up spontaneously, filling the room with warmth. My best friend leaned closer, cradling my belly like a fragile treasure. She cooed in a playful baby voice, *"You like the name your auntie gave you? Yes, you do!"* The laughter, the love, and the connection we shared in that moment were indescribable.

As the night drew close, I felt an overwhelming sense of completeness. In that cocoon of laughter and love, I realized I was having a son named Landon. The origin of Landon's name is a cherished and enduring memory. Weeks of worry dissolved into a tranquil joy as I slept, dreaming of Landon, our soon-to-be-born son.

CHAPTER *1*

My Little Birdie to a Diagnosis

Nurturing Joy, Enduring Heartbreak: A Dual Odyssey

The moment my son, Landon, was born—right on his due date, March 1, 2007—felt nothing short of miraculous. The hospital room buzzed with the sounds of beeping monitors and joyful conversation, yet all I could focus on was the life I was about to meet. After 21 hours and 43 minutes of labor, every contraction heightened my anticipation. I was exhausted, but the thought of finally holding him gave me strength.

As 11:15 p.m. approached, my heart pounded—it was finally time to push. Labor had tested me in ways I never could have imagined, but I was ready. With my son's father, sister, and mother by my side, the doctor's steady voice broke through my fog of fatigue, offering encouragement with each push. My sister kept updating me, saying, *"I can see his head! You're so close; keep going!"* Everyone was urging me to deliver him before midnight so he could be born on his due date. It felt like the room had transformed into a stadium filled with excited fans.

After what felt like an eternity of pain and exhaustion, Landon made his grand entrance into the world at 11:43 p.m., and the room erupted into motion.

He weighed six pounds, fifteen ounces, and measured 20.5 inches long. The Apgar scores—9 and 9—brought a rush of relief: my baby was healthy. But as the nurse cared for him, I was suddenly overcome. My body trembled with postpartum shakes, and though I ached to hold him, I couldn't.

Then our eyes met, and the rest of the world faded. The noise, the lights, the pain, the chaos—they all vanished. In that instant, love crashed over me, potent and pure. I couldn't believe he was mine. This delicate, beautiful little person was my son. He was perfect. I wasn't just someone who had gone through labor anymore—I was a mother. It felt like he had always been mine like we had known each other long before that night. Landon's soft cries filled the room, each one carrying the promise of stories to read, steps to take, words to speak, and memories to make.

When I finally steadied myself, I held him close, our breathing in perfect rhythm. It was a moment I'll never forget; his warm body resting against my chest, his tiny hand wrapped around my finger. Everything else became a blur. We were just two people who belonged to each other.

But too soon, the medical team took him for his newborn assessments: screening, fingerprinting, taking footprints, and a full cleaning before he could be brought to the nursery. I watched them carry him away; my heart tugged in a dozen directions—pride, love, and a flicker of worry. Would he be okay? I already missed him.

While the medical team cared for him, I was taken to my maternity room to clean up and rest, while his dad stayed by his side. As I settled into bed, the room's quietness allowed me to absorb the greatest moment of my life. I could still feel the warmth of my son's skin, my breath syncing instinctively with his. As I drifted off, the thought "I am a mom, Landon's mom" consumed my mind and filled my heart.

A few hours later, around 3:30 a.m., a soft knock pulled me from a light sleep. I opened my eyes—and there he was. My sweet baby boy, Landon, swaddled tightly in a soft white blanket and wearing a blue knitted hat in his

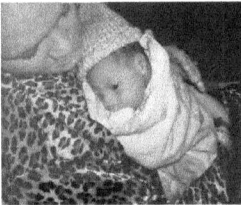

bassinet. In that quiet moment, I was in awe, staring at his perfect little face, ready to feed and bond. The room was hushed, the hospital's ambient hum oddly soothing. I felt an overwhelming gratitude for this brief window of calm alone with him, knowing that visitors would soon fill the room. It was a moment I tucked into my heart, knowing I'd carry it forever.

Throughout the day, a steady stream of family and 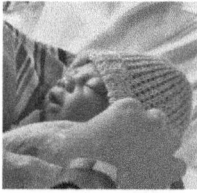 friends brought joy and celebration. But beneath it all, his father and I sensed something was off. Landon struggled with feeding—he would latch, then pull away, his face tightening in discomfort. His breathing was heavy, and soft, pained moans made our hearts ache. We voiced our concerns to the nurse, who gently reassured us that newborns often have small hiccups in their first days. Still, when she took him for an exam, I held my breath and asked, *"Is my baby okay?"*

"He's healthy, but we'll have the doctor take a look," the nurse replied. However, the tension in her face conveyed more than her words, or perhaps it was my anxiety that perceived it that way. Relief trickled in when they returned Landon to my room, saying everything looked fine. I held him close, clinging to the peace that moment offered.

As night came and exhaustion set in, I nervously agreed to send Landon to the nursery. I hoped we'd both get some rest before introducing him to our quiet, love-filled life at home. My heart fluttered at the thought—but sleep felt necessary.

That hope shattered at 1 a.m. A loud knock startled me awake. I threw back the sheets and stood quickly, expecting to see my son—but it wasn't Landon at the door. It was a team of doctors, their faces marked with concern. A cold rush went through me.

"Hi, Mom, we need to talk about Landon's condition," one of them said gently. My chest tightened. Panic rose in my throat. Tears welled up and fell before I even understood what was being said.

"He's been admitted to the NICU. He's in good hands."

The NICU was a world of hope and heartbreak, where tiny lives battled quietly behind glass. Just twenty-three hours after his birth, I wasn't holding Landon, I was watching a team of specialists' work to keep him stable. Seeing his tiny body connected to wires and machines shattered me. Each beep echoed through me like a warning bell, an unrelenting reminder of how fragile life can be.

As days blurred into what felt like endless hours, I spent every waking moment in the NICU. The nurses became my anchors, patiently explaining every beep and alarm on the monitors. They offered brief but vital glimpses of progress amid the uncertainty. I slowly learned the language of this strange new world— *"His oxygen saturation is improving,"* they'd say, and I'd finally let out a breath I didn't realize I was holding. Every small improvement felt monumental, each one a quiet step forward.

But the nights were the hardest. Knowing he was alone in that incubator, fighting through respiratory distress, pulmonary hypertension, meconium aspiration, low muscle tone, and low oxygen levels—tore at something deep inside me.

At home, the silence was louder than anything. I'd curl up in the rocking chair in his sports-themed nursery, holding the blanket my sister handmade for him, breathing in the faint scent of baby detergent and the dreams I had woven into every fold. I envisioned cradling him to sleep, whispering bedtime stories, and feeling the weight of his tiny body in my arms. Instead, I found myself staring at an empty room, praying that my son would continue to pull through.

In the middle of it all, I was especially grateful to my sister and one of my best friends. They were constants in the chaos—showing up at the hospital every day without question. They brought laughter, fresh clothes, food, and moments of calm when everything else felt frayed. Their presence softened the edges of my grief, their compassion reminding me that we weren't alone.

Our wider circle of family and friends many of whom had held Landon before he was admitted—wrapped us in steady support. They checked in, sent messages, and offered prayers. Each note, each call, each prayer—was a lifeline. Their care gave us strength on even the heaviest days, helping us hold onto the belief that we would bring our son home soon.

Each night, I whispered silent prayers, picturing Landon growing stronger. Then one morning, something felt different the moment I stepped into the NICU. The familiar hum of machines filled the room, but the air held a lighter energy. My eyes searched quickly, landing on his incubator.

As I approached, my heart pounded. *"He's stable today,"* the nurse said gently, *"and we've started weaning him off the oxygen."* I froze. Her words were so close but felt so distant. The moment felt like a dream.

Leaning over, I watched him blink beneath the soft lights. His bluish-gray eyes met mine—eyes that seemed to see straight into my soul. In that moment, everything else faded. It was just the two of us, bound by something beyond language. A silent promise.

One day, I heard, *"Mom, would you like to hold your son?"* At first, I couldn't tell if those words were a figment of my imagination or a whisper from my heart. The moment I had been waiting for finally came. His light weight and warm presence reassured me it was real, not a dream. I marveled at his tiny features—his soft skin, his reflex smiles, and the faintest flutter of his eyelids.

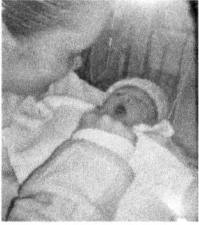

"Look at you, my little fighter," I whispered, my voice trembling with emotion. At that moment, I no longer saw him as just a patient, confined by the limitations of his fragile state; I saw my son—a living embodiment of hope, resilience, and love. Each soft sound he made, whether a gentle sigh or a fleeting whimper, resonated with strength. Each small milestone—breathing without assistance and taking his first feed—felt like a quiet miracle.

The NICU—once a place of fear and uncertainty—slowly became a space filled with something else: hope. I watched my son grow stronger each day, and with every breath he took, I found my own strength building alongside his. We held onto each other—quietly, fiercely—waiting for the day we could finally bring our brave little boy home, ready to fill our lives with laughter and light.

Driving home, a new kind of weight lifted from my chest. I realized then that motherhood wasn't one path but many, and I would need to draw on every ounce of strength I had to stand by my son. The road ahead wouldn't be easy, but I wasn't alone. Whatever came next, Landon and I would face it together—one heartbeat at a time.

The Long-Awaited Arrival: Bringing Him Home

Before Landon was born, life felt like a whirlwind I couldn't quite catch up with. The day after my baby shower, I developed bronchitis and battled it for over two weeks, with each cough rattling my already stretched body. Being eight and a half months pregnant made everything feel heavier, sharper, and more fragile. When I finally saw my doctor, the visit brought something tangible: antibiotics to fight the infection and Ambien to help me sleep.

I trusted my doctor completely. It never occurred to me to question the combination of medications I'd been given. But after Landon's birth, when the complications unfolded, I found myself circling back. The Ambien haunted me. I later read of possible links between medication and newborn distress. Guilt came in hard and fast—waves crashing into my chest without warning. I couldn't stop asking myself: What if I hadn't taken it? Would things have been different? Why didn't I research the effects medication could have on my unborn son?

But the past couldn't be rewritten. Instead of drowning in regret, I chose to treat that experience as a turning point. A lesson. One I would carry forward with purpose and caution.

Through all of it, gratitude anchored me. The NICU team—nurses, doctors, specialists, and other parents—were extraordinary. Their quiet dedication, care, and compassion reminded me daily that Landon was in the best hands possible. I watched his progress with awe: breathing on his own, tolerating feedings, becoming more alert. Each step forward was a quiet victory.

Then came March 7, 2007.

That day, surrounded by a NICU doctor, a cardiologist, and a neurologist, I heard the words I had waited so long to hear, *"Landon can go home tomorrow as he is stable and doing well. Please bring the car seat inside when you arrive to take him home."* The mix of joy, disbelief, and relief hit me all at once. As I stepped outside the hospital that night, my body flooded with emotion. Tomorrow, I would bring my baby boy home.

That night, I couldn't sit still. I dove into full-on nesting mode—preparing his coming home outfit, ensuring the car seat was safely installed, reorganizing the nursery, smoothing out fresh linens, double-checking every diaper, box of wipes, and pacifier. My heart felt light. Thoughts of holding Landon in his room, watching him sleep in his bassinet and crib, flooded my mind. My prayers were answered. Sleep, for me, was impossible. All I could think about was the life we were about to begin—together, at home.

The next morning, I returned to the hospital, my heart pounding with a mix of anticipation and nerves. This was the day I had longed for through six days of visits filled with uncertainty. As I walked the familiar NICU corridors one final time, waves of emotion surged—gratitude, anxiety, and pure joy all crashing at once. Landon's godfather, who came to support us, noticed the tension building in me. With a reassuring smile, he said, *"Let's go get your baby boy, my godson, and bring him home."* His words wrapped around me like a warm blanket, reminding me that love surrounded us.

Seeing Landon again was overwhelming in the most beautiful way. My heart swelled as I dressed him for the first—and last—time in the hospital. A sense of peace settled over me, softening the weight I had carried for too long. Before we left, the NICU staff walked us through his progress, answered our lingering questions, and explained the care he would need in the coming weeks.

Finally stepping out of the hospital and placing him in the car felt surreal. I had waited a lifetime for that moment. It was the second happiest day of my life—etched in my memory as the beginning of everything we had fought for. We were going home.

After Landon's long-awaited arrival, our home transformed into a lively hub filled with laughter as friends and family came to meet him, both for the first time and once again. Among the crowd was his godfather, who surprised me by bringing my cousin—a vibrant woman whose laughter brightened the room. We hadn't seen each other in ages and embracing her filled my heart with nostalgia.

The connection was palpable as she sat beside me, gazing at Landon, her baby cousin, for the first time. Her eyes sparkled with affection as she cooed at him while offering a smile to me that spoke louder than words. I pondered over nicknames that would suit their bond, but none seemed to capture the beauty of the moment. Then, as if reading my thoughts, she lovingly called him "wittle tiny." A week after being home with family and friends, he received his first nickname, and I knew that moment would lead to more firsts worth capturing.

A Journey Through His First Years at Home

During Landon's first year, each day unfolded like a brand-new adventure, packed with milestones that sparked joy and wonder. From the start, he had a way of capturing my attention—whether it was his soft coos from the crib, his continuous raspberries during a car ride, or how his wide, curious eyes lit up every time he spotted my face.

As the months passed, I found myself eagerly awaiting every new "first." The day he rolled over felt like a celebration; I clapped and cheered, and his delighted giggles filled the room. It was just the beginning. Sitting up came next—he wobbled, laughed, and tried again, undeterred by every little tumble.

Of course, there were not-so-good times—like those pesky colds that seemed to come out of nowhere. On those days, I'd pace the floor, rocking him gently, whispering words of comfort while he clung to me. Yet, even then, there was a brightness in his eyes that never dimmed. He'd look up with a small smile, showing me that his spirit was stronger than anything that came his way.

One rainy afternoon, we sat by the window, watching raindrops race down the glass. I rested my hand on his back while he pointed outside, and I softly sang *"The Itsy-Bitsy Spider."* The joy on his face made the room feel warmer.

As he grew more mobile, curiosity turned into exploration. We'd spend hours playing on the carpet, where he took his first wobbly steps. He clapped, babbled, and shrieked with laughter as he moved from place to place, delighted by every new discovery.

I was constantly captivated by his personality—the way he pointed at things that fascinated him, the spontaneous dancing, the cheerful clapping, and his infectious laugh. One memory I treasure deeply: whenever I said *"cheese,"* his whole face would light up with a radiant smile even without a camera present. That joy reflected the bond we shared—timeless and true.

The day Landon first called me *"Mama"* —at just nine months—is one I'll never forget. It was more than a milestone. It was recognition. I smiled, heart full, and whispered, *"That's right, baby, I am."* In that quiet moment, the world faded. It was just the two of us, surrounded by a love deeper than words.

By the time his first birthday arrived, Landon was a whirlwind of energy—babbling, crawling, and exploring every corner of our home. I threw a big party to celebrate the year we had journeyed through. Family gathered, laughter echoed, and his cake—covered in bright Sesame Street colors—was ready for him to dive into. Though he was startled by the Elmo character dancing at his party and surprised by the burst of everyone singing *"Happy Birthday,"* the sight of his smile and frosting-covered face after he took his first bite is etched in my heart. A moment of pure, messy joy.

Yet our journey wasn't without trials. In those early years, Landon faced a series of health challenges. From chickenpox to croup, ear infections to pneumonia, it often felt like a never-ending cycle of appointments, hospital visits, and treatments. He battled thrush, tear duct infections, pink eye, upper respiratory illnesses, unexplained viruses— even Coxsackie virus. Some days were filled with worry, especially when allergic reactions or gastrointestinal issues appeared out of nowhere.

Hospital visits and pediatrician appointments became sources of anxiety rather than the joy they once brought—seeing how much he'd grown or how much he weighed. But we faced each challenge together, and in doing so, our bond grew stronger. Those difficult moments made the bright ones feel even more meaningful.

Everything Can Change in the Blink of an Eye

It was an otherwise ordinary day in March 2008. Rain tapped gently on the windows as I got Landon ready for his doctor's appointment. At twelve and a half months old, it was time for his scheduled vaccinations. I felt a mix of anxiety and hesitation. The thought of him having three shots totaling five viruses in one day seemed a bit much. I hated seeing him cry after shots and I worried that his little body couldn't handle them, but I knew the MMR, Hep A, and tuberculin vaccines were important.

Still, something felt off. I couldn't explain it, but a sense of unease lingered—like I was coming down with something. Perhaps it was the rain that drizzled outside, creating a gloomy backdrop to our morning, or maybe it was my rising anxiety. Whatever it was, I couldn't shake the nagging feeling that today was different.

As I bundled Landon into his jacket, I tried to focus on the positive aspects of our outing. *"You'll be so brave today, my little man,"* I said, squeezing his tiny hand. He smiled back at me, unaware of the uncertainty within me. Like all kids, Landon needed vaccinations to protect him from various illnesses. However, after receiving several shots in the past, things had taken an unexpected turn.

We arrived at the doctor, the scent of antiseptic permeating the air. I watched as Landon played with the toys in the waiting room, his laughter momentarily easing my fears. However, the memory of his previous post-vaccination woes crept back into my mind. Although many children experience typical post-vaccination fatigue, Landon often felt quite unwell. After his last few shots, he developed symptoms, including high fevers, rashes, and lethargy. Concerned, I would rush him to the doctor, only to find out that he was dealing with a virus unrelated to the vaccinations.

There were instances of tear duct issues, bouts of pink eye that caused his eyes to itch and water uncontrollably, and even croup that had him barking like a seal in the middle of the night. The pattern was the same almost each time: one problem after another, all surfacing shortly after his vaccine appointments. After a particularly tough visit, during which eczema flared up and left his skin red and itchy following his third round of the Hepatitis B shot, I expressed my concerns to the doctor once again.

"Are you sure this isn't related to the vaccines? It seems that after he receives a shot, more often than not, something happens," I asked, feeling dread. With a warm and understanding smile, his doctor reassured me that these issues were unrelated to the vaccinations. *"These things happen, and vaccines are important for his health,"* he explained.

My anxiety grew as Landon received his vaccinations one by one, but I was thankful the appointment went smoothly. Landon handled the shots with less fuss. We came home, and I kept busy with housework while keeping an eye on him. He started walking and loved to explore the house independently but followed me everywhere. My heart filled with joy each time he took one step more than the last before falling. But five hours later, my heart began to pound. He looked at me in a daze as I cradled him in my arms. Then, without warning, his body went stiff. He started seizing.

He convulsed in my arms while his father called 911. My body shook as panic surged through me. When the paramedics arrived, their calm presence offered a sliver of relief. They immediately carried him to the ambulance while I explained he had been fine just hours earlier. As we raced to the hospital, I felt like novocaine had numbed my body. It was hard for me to distinguish whether it was a dream or real. He seized for sixteen minutes and spiked a 105.1 fever following his episode.

At the hospital, the medical team moved quickly. They checked his vitals, performed an EKG, gave him Tylenol, connected him to an IV, and ran blood tests. Soon after, Landon underwent an EEG to monitor brain activity. Each beep and hum from the machines intensified my fear.

Yet the team's steady hands and quiet professionalism reminded me that he was in good care.

Hours later, two senior staff members approached. Their expressions were gentle but serious. Before they spoke, I sensed the gravity of what was coming. They confirmed that Landon had experienced an adverse reaction to the vaccinations and explained the need for state-mandated reporting.

My heart sank. Still, I appreciated their transparency during such a traumatic moment.

After completing the paperwork, I found myself still struggling to make sense of everything. I approached one of the nurses, hoping for more clarity. She listened patiently, answered my questions, and reassured me that everything was proceeding with protocol. Her calmness grounded me. I needed that.

That night, as we prepared to leave, a swirl of emotions overtook me—confusion, relief, fear, gratitude. Landon was back in my arms. He was okay. But reality lingered: life could change in an instant. I stepped into the night air with him close to my chest, thankful for the care we received and hopeful that better days lay ahead.

Discovering the Signs of Autism

At first, I didn't think much of it. I didn't even know what to call it. About ten days after the hospital visit, I noticed something new.

It was a cool evening, and the scent of fried chicken filled our kitchen. Rihanna's *"Please Don't Stop the Music"* played in the background. Landon's laughter echoed through the house, and we danced together, letting the music move us.

When I set him down to check the stove, I turned and saw him flapping his hands and spinning in circles, his face glowing with delight. It was mesmerizing. His hands moved like tiny wings, fluttering in sync with his excitement.

"Keep dancing, baby! You're amazing!" I cheered, watching his joy light up the room.

He continued the motion throughout the evening— pure, unfiltered joy. It was new. Something I hadn't seen in him before or other children. But I didn't feel concerned. His happiness was contagious, and I found myself mimicking his moves as we danced together.

Still, a quiet question took root in the back of my mind. Why does he do that? Is it just a dance? A new way of showing excitement? I couldn't name it, but the thought lingered.

Over the next few days, I noticed the movement more often. One quiet April evening, after tucking Landon into bed, I sat in the stillness of our home. He lay peacefully beneath the covers. But inside me, something had shifted. A sense of weight pressed against my chest—a growing awareness I couldn't yet define.

I couldn't shake the image of his hand movements—so unique and expressive, like a bird flapping its wings. His excitement and frustration radiated through those gestures, and while they were captivating, they also began to trouble me.

Driven by a desperate need to understand, I turned on my computer and typed, "my son moves his hands like a bird." My fingers trembled as I hit enter. A knot tightened in my stomach as anxiety surged. Almost instantly, the screen filled with results—articles, blogs, research studies—all circling the same topic: autism. Many even referenced Rain Man—a movie I'd seen before, but never fully grasped.

As I scrolled through the page, my heart sank. Could Landon be on the autism spectrum? A whirlwind of thoughts swirled. Would he be able to navigate everyday life? Make friends? Be accepted for who he is, not judged for how he's different? Would he ever get his words back? Would he ever live independently or have his own family one day? Most of all, would he get the chance to discover and pursue his dreams without limitation?

With each article I read, the worry deepened. A wave of empathy swept over me—not just for my son, but for every family who had walked this uncertain path. The thought of Landon facing hardship broke something in me. It pressed down hard, and in a moment of overwhelm, I powered down the computer. I needed space from the fear threatening to consume me.

That night, I climbed into bed and hoped for rest, but sleep wouldn't come. My mind raced with questions. The dark felt heavier than usual—weighted with uncertainty and concern for my son's future. A tightness settled in my chest, a quiet voice whispering that something wasn't right. I clung to the hope that what I was seeing were simply harmless quirks, not signs of something more serious.

Days passed, but my unease didn't fade. I lived in a space between denial and reality, wanting to protect Landon from everything, while slowly facing the possibility of a difficult truth. It was a space no parent wants to live in—clouded with doubt, fear, and love all at once.

One day, standing beside him, I was hit by a surge of love so overwhelming it seemed to wrap around both of us. But alongside that love was fear—deep, quiet, and constant.

I felt caught in an emotional tug-of-war, my heart and mind pulling in opposite directions. I was lost. I was petrified. All I could do was hold onto a fragile thread of hope and optimism, praying it would guide us through the unknown.

Signs That Grew Louder

Over time, I began to notice something heartbreaking: many of the words Landon used to say began to disappear. Words like "outside," "I stink," "dancing," "apple," "car," "cheese," "truck," and "baba" slowly faded. In their place came frustration—tears, tantrums, and sounds I couldn't understand. I struggled to connect, to interpret what he needed. And that helplessness hurt.

At first, I tried not to overthink it. But his lack of engagement and difficulty communicating became impossible to ignore. He no longer pointed or responded to his name. He moaned, hummed, cried, hit, rocked, banged his head, picked at his skin, scratched, and occasionally bite. I knew I needed to say something.

The Endless War

Bringing it up to the pediatrician wasn't easy. Anxiety churned in my stomach, but I couldn't hold it in any longer. The doctor reassured me that it was common for kids to lose some abilities while gaining new ones. I tried to believe him. I was new to all of this— a first-time mom. His words brought some relief, but the hand-flapping still echoed in my mind. Something felt off.

A few weeks later, I made another appointment. My concerns had grown. Landon wasn't just losing words—he was replacing skills with behaviors I hadn't seen before. He stopped sharing what he found interesting. He reacted oddly to noises and textures. Small changes in his routine caused big reactions.

Again, I voiced my concerns. Again, the doctor brushed them aside. *"He's fine,"* he told me. *"It's normal. You're just a first-time panicking mom. It seems you are trying to find something that simply isn't there."*

I left the office that day feeling defeated—as if I were failing my son. The doctor's words stayed with me, pressing against my chest, even as I tried to focus on everything else that needed my attention.

But something else awakened in me that day—a quiet fire. A fierce need to advocate for Landon. I didn't have any answers, but I knew I had to fight for him. That moment marked the beginning of a journey I hadn't expected: a path of determination. A journey to ensure my son would be seen, understood, and supported for exactly who he was.

After many months of persistence, I finally secured a referral for my son to receive a full speech evaluation and a comprehensive hearing test. When the hearing results came back normal, I felt a brief wave of relief—but it didn't last long. As I expected, the evaluation revealed a mild speech delay. Mild? I thought. He's not talking anymore.

The medical team decided not to pursue further assessments at that point. They emphasized the importance of allowing him time to develop at his own pace, reminding me that he was still very young.

During this process, I struggled to find the right words to express my growing concerns. My frustration deepened with each visit, especially as it became clear that the pediatrician couldn't offer the direction I so desperately needed.

I cried for days, feeling the disconnection that consumed me, separating me from my truth. I was left feeling stranded—disappointed, disheartened, and at times, utterly defeated.

Still, I knew I had to keep searching. The weight of hopelessness was real, but I couldn't let it stop me. My journey wasn't over.

Each day, I put on a brave face, masking the chaos swirling inside. My thoughts spiraled endlessly, tangled in a storm I couldn't control. It felt like the walls were closing in, and the isolation wrapped around me like a heavy fog. I longed for connection but felt trapped.

Guilt crept in. Was I wrong to question what everyone else had dismissed? I thought. The doctor had repeatedly told me there was nothing wrong, but I couldn't ignore what I saw and felt. I began to doubt myself, questioning my instincts, wondering if I was somehow failing as a mother.

Month after month, my son was labeled "fine." Eventually, I stopped bringing up my concerns. It felt pointless. Every time I asked for further evaluation, more tests, or a specialist, I was met with denial or delay. Each dismissal chipped away at my confidence. I was tired of not being heard, feeling powerless, and being treated like I didn't know my own child.

But deep down, even when the world told me to stop, I knew I had to keep pushing. I realized no one knew my son the way I did—and no one else was going to fight for him the way I would, but I was going in circles. No one was listening or taking this seriously. I felt lost and broken at times, so I gave up.

When I say, "I gave up," it doesn't mean I ignored the situation—far from it. Instead, I stopped trying to engage with the pediatrician and chose to observe my son closely while immersing myself in research. Each appointment became a silent struggle. I longed to speak up, but I held back, waiting for something concrete. I believed that pouring my complicated thoughts into a conversation with someone unwilling to listen would be fruitless.

I made a conscious effort to see things from the doctor's point of view. I often reassured myself that maybe he had valid reasons, that perhaps my concerns were exaggerated or unfounded. It was possible. I reasoned that he simply lacked deep experience with autism—something that might explain his resistance. This internal dialogue helped me process my emotions, even as I questioned whether I was misreading signs that felt all too clear to me.

But as time passed, it became harder to ignore what I was seeing. The doctor didn't just disagree with me—he dismissed me. He failed to make room for a deeper conversation, one that could have focused on my son's unique needs. What I needed wasn't just answers—I needed someone to truly listen.

A genuine dialogue might have opened a door to insight, partnership, and better care. Instead, I learned something I hadn't expected: that compassion and empathy are just as vital in medicine as expertise.

Deep down, I knew I understood my son in a way no one else could. What a doctor saw in fifteen minutes could never compare to what I lived with every day. The fear that continued inaction would stifle his development pushed me forward. Even if I sounded irrational to others, I couldn't afford to wait. So, I did what I could. I threw myself into research—hours upon hours of reading about autism, special needs, treatments, strategies, and how best to support Landon as he learned, socialized, and adjusted to the world around him. The library and local bookstore were my second home.

By February 2009, my frustration had reached a tipping point. I called my insurance provider to see what options were available. I was ready to pursue help from a specialist—a pediatric neurologist or a developmental pediatrician—regardless of cost and whether his doctor approved.

After a brief hold, I spoke with a compassionate, understanding and knowledgeable representative whose calm voice immediately put me at ease. She walked me through my benefits explaining that our PPO plan didn't require a referral to see a specialist. I felt relieved. For the first time in a long while, I felt empowered.

Along with discussing my options for seeing a specialist, the representative also encouraged me to contact our state's early intervention program. Because my son was under the age of three, she explained he would qualify for an evaluation. I was relieved and grateful to learn that the program didn't require a referral or insurance, making it accessible for families like ours. If he qualified for services, they would be provided at no cost or based on a sliding scale determined by our household income. That news renewed my hope and strengthened my determination to advocate for my son. I promised myself that no outside pressure or discouragement would shake my resolve.

It was clear Landon was trying to communicate something important through his behaviors, and I refused to ignore that. Every day, I reminded myself that my voice was the only one he had—until he found his own. I would no longer stay silent or be gaslighted, no matter the obstacles ahead.

With a new sense of purpose, I reached out to the early intervention program, and they scheduled an evaluation for March 2009. I also began calling pediatric neurologists and developmental pediatricians to ask about availability, explaining the reasons for my inquiry.

I was eager for expert insight into my son's development. I'd grown weary of the advice to "wait and see." I needed practical guidance to better understand his needs and to make sure I was doing everything I could. The uncertainty was wearing on me, and I longed for clarity to move forward with confidence.

After a series of phone calls, I learned the earliest available appointment with a pediatric neurologist was in May 2009. The wait felt endless. Still, I reminded myself that we were moving forward—closer to the answers we needed. I knew finding the right specialist was crucial, so we booked the appointment, carrying a mix of hope and apprehension.

A few weeks after my initial call, the Early Intervention team came to our home. The evaluation lasted about two hours and involved interactive activities as the specialist observed Landon's responses and interactions.

After the assessment, they determined Landon had a 33% delay in both speech and language skills. This matched my early concerns and qualified him for speech therapy. I believed this support could build not only his communication but also his confidence.

While I was thankful for the services, I felt disappointed that they didn't recommend support in other areas. Although his scores in those domains fell within age-appropriate ranges, I still found it hard to accept. They encouraged me to keep monitoring his progress and to reach out if I noticed regression or ongoing delays. Why was no one seeing what I saw clearly? I couldn't understand.

A few weeks later, still concerned, I contacted Early Intervention again and requested a reevaluation—this time focusing on potential occupational, behavioral, and physical therapy. I described troubling signs: loss of speech, uncoordinated movements, sensory challenges, feeding difficulties, emerging harmful behaviors, and noticeable delays in both fine and gross motor skills.

Despite sharing these detailed observations, my request for OT, PT and behavioral therapy was denied. However, I was informed that he qualified for once-weekly developmental intervention therapy, which would help monitor his progress and provide tailored support. It wasn't the full range of services I'd hoped for, but I remained optimistic that this intervention could still make a meaningful difference.

In May 2009, Landon began receiving weekly speech and developmental intervention therapy at home and in daycare. While the limited services didn't fully meet my expectations, I was genuinely grateful for the therapists' professionalism and care. Their patience, attentiveness, and deep understanding of child development were evident in every session.

The staff at the daycare was outstanding and welcomed the therapists with open arms. Both the staff and the therapists consistently communicated Landon's daily progress to me through reports and face-to-face conversations. Most importantly, they saw Landon as an individual, not just his diagnosis, and helped him develop skills in language, motor skills, and social interactions. To this day, I am extremely grateful that they were part of his journey.

Over time, I saw real growth in Landon's speech, language comprehension—expressive and receptive, and motor skills. His confidence began to bloom, and I felt immense joy watching him express himself more clearly and connect more with the world around him. Still, I remained aware of the developmental challenges he faced, along with new concerns that continued to surface.

Despite my efforts to voice my concerns, I encountered growing resistance the more I sought support. Many of the higher level professionals involved were focused on identifying only significant delays, and during their brief assessments, they often failed to observe the behaviors that most concerned me.

Sometimes, they dismissed my observations as age-appropriate, which left me increasingly frustrated. Each time I raised concerns; I was reassured that he was developing within normal limits and encouraged to simply "wait and see."

But the notion that my son had to face more severe challenges before he could access meaningful help felt deeply wrong. I believed in the value of early support and understood that even small steps could lead to meaningful progress.

It often felt like I was trapped in a waking nightmare—trying to do what I believed was right for my son yet constantly second-guessing whether his struggles were truly atypical or if I was overreacting. I wrestled with the tension between trusting my instincts and the fear of making things harder for him.

We attended playground outings and "mommy and me" classes, where he had other structured opportunities to engage with other children. Yet outside of these moments, I had few chances to truly observe how his development compared with his peers.

Family gatherings didn't offer the same lens—they were limited in scope and didn't provide much insight into how children his age typically behaved. As a result, I often felt unsure about his progress in areas like language, motor skills, and social interaction.

I understood that comparing children isn't always ideal, but I also believed that some comparisons were necessary. After all, doctors use standardized growth charts, developmental checklists, and vaccination schedules—why couldn't I use similar reference points to make sense of what I was seeing?

I needed context, especially when it came to social skills and milestones. Even if the method wasn't perfect, having some frame of reference helped guide my parenting decisions.

Through these observations, I began noticing patterns: his preference for solitary or parallel play, his tendency to line up or spin objects, irregular sleep habits, and his sensitivity to disruptions—loud noises, temperature changes, shifts in routine, clothing textures, or certain foods.

He showed visible signs of anxiety, especially when his hands got dirty—grimacing and pulling away as if recoiling from an unseen threat. Grass triggered a similar response; he would cling tightly to me, as if the ground itself posed danger. Thunderstorms terrified him, his small frame shaking at the sound of thunder, though the rain that followed seemed to soothe him.

In social spaces, he approached other children—and even toys—with hesitation, as if unsure whether they were safe. Objects that once brought him joy, like bath toys, began to cause distress, as if they now held the power to harm.

His clinginess intensified in unfamiliar settings or around new people. He'd press into me with a grip that felt both desperate and heartbreaking, like he was trying to anchor himself against a world that felt too big, too fast, and too unpredictable.

The fear Landon experienced was palpable—an all-consuming anxiety shaped by both what he could understand and what lay beyond his grasp. These episodes often spiraled into meltdowns, his frustration erupting in distressing and sometimes heartbreaking ways.

His loss of speech and limited ability to express his emotions only intensified the struggle. He couldn't explain the turmoil inside and my heart broke as I tried to make sense of it all. Each day felt like an emotional puzzle, with me trying to piece together the fragments of his distress.

This led me to focus intensely on every detail—his behavior, his body language, and the environment we moved through. I became hyperaware, constantly interpreting his reactions and searching for meaning in his silences. In the swirl of uncertainty and anxiety, my mission became clear: to build a sense of safety within the chaos. I wanted to create a space where he could feel calm, understood, and protected.

As I grappled with the unknowns surrounding Landon's condition, I also wrestled with what it meant to truly support him. Though I had doubts about the guidance I was receiving, I accepted the limited services being offered and their set frequency. But emotionally, I couldn't accept the idea that this was enough.

While we waited for the neurologist appointment, I kept searching for ways to help him at home—anything that might complement the services in place. Deep down, I sensed he needed more, even if I couldn't pinpoint exactly what that was. Despite my continued advocacy, it often felt like I was standing still, making no visible progress.

Watching him struggle filled me with a sorrow I hadn't known before. I began questioning myself as a mother—wondering if I was doing enough, or if I was somehow failing him. I was reaching a breaking point, emotionally drained from the constant waiting, rejection, gaslighting, and self-doubt.

I realized I needed to pause and take care of myself. I couldn't support him fully if I was running on empty. In moments of quiet reflection, I gave myself permission to rest—to gather the strength I would need to keep going. I promised myself that when the neurologist's appointment finally arrived, I would try to accept it if nothing concerning was found. But if there was something—anything—I would return to the fight with an even greater resolve.

To reclaim a sense of peace, I returned to journaling and reading at night. Stories had always brought me comfort, and I found solace in the voices of others. One afternoon at Barnes & Noble, I came across a book that hit close to home: Louder Than Words by Jenny McCarthy. As I read, I cried. Her story mirrored mine in many ways, offering validation and clarity when I needed it most.

McCarthy's words helped me put our experience into perspective and articulate what I hadn't been able to fully express. I felt deep compassion for her and her son, even as I recognized how our journeys differed. Her book gave me more than comfort—it gave me a sense of connection. It reminded me that we weren't alone, that countless families were navigating similar terrain. And in that shared struggle, I found motivation to keep moving forward, to keep breaking the cycle that held so many of us back.

The Final Battle: A Journey Towards Inner Harmony

Ahead of Landon's appointment with the neurologist, I found renewed motivation to continue researching autism, child development, vaccinations, and various forms of therapy. I carefully documented my observations—his behaviors, preferences, strengths, and the challenges he faced day to day.

I believed that a deeper understanding would allow me to communicate our experience more clearly and confidently. I spent countless hours reading at home, visiting libraries, and browsing bookstores—immersing myself in the complexities of autism: its possible causes, symptoms, variations in severity, therapeutic options, and long-term considerations. Research grounded me.

I focused on the five distinct diagnostic categories and began to see patterns that aligned closely with Pervasive Developmental Disorder-Not Otherwise Specified (PDD-NOS). Landon exhibited limited social interaction, difficulty with verbal and nonverbal communication, and repetitive behaviors and interests. Discovering that these traits fit within an established diagnosis helped me feel less alone in what we were experiencing. It also gave me a sense of direction—I felt prepared to speak with the neurologist, bringing not only my observations but also informed questions and ideas for how to help my son thrive.

On May 15, 2009, following a thorough evaluation that lasted nearly three hours, the neurologist confirmed a diagnosis of autism—specifically, Pervasive Developmental Disorder-Not Otherwise Specified (PDD-NOS) with sensory challenges. At that time, PDD-NOS was classified as part of the broader autism spectrum, prior to the 2013 changes that consolidated multiple diagnoses under autism spectrum disorder (ASD).

The neurologist explained that while Landon exhibited many signs consistent with autism, he didn't meet the full criteria for either classic autism or Asperger's syndrome, making his diagnosis more nuanced. She also shared that as Landon continued to grow and develop, his symptoms might evolve, and his diagnosis could shift accordingly.

She recommended follow-up visits—six months later and then annually—to monitor his progress and adjust support as needed. Before we left, she took a moment to acknowledge my efforts. She commended my advocacy, stating that children like Landon benefit significantly from parents who act promptly and stay engaged in their care.

In that moment, her words comforted me. After nearly a year of exhaustion, doubt, and emotional numbness, I felt seen—not only as a mother, but as a person trying to do her best under extraordinary circumstances. I left her office feeling informed, encouraged, and united in our purpose to support Landon as fully as possible.

I became vigilant in observing my son's behaviors and developmental changes, continuing to study autism and its ongoing influence on his growth, even to this day. I never doubted that something was wrong. Still, our pediatrician urged me to downplay my concerns. Even as I noticed clear signs of regression and persistent delays, I was repeatedly told that he was "fine" because he had once met certain early milestones.

I'll always be deeply grateful to Landon's neurologist. She was the doctor he truly needed. The day he received his autism diagnosis is one I'll never forget. It may sound unusual, but that moment brought me comfort, hope, and peace. After so much uncertainty, it reassured me that I wasn't imagining things.

The diagnosis validated my instincts and gave me the language to explain what I'd been seeing for so long. Someone finally heard me—someone saw Landon the way I did. That recognition allowed me to better support him and affirmed that all the love, effort, and persistence I had poured into motherhood hadn't been in vain. I was exactly where I needed to be—right beside him, every step of the way.

The day after the diagnosis, I felt an unexpected calm. The emotional weight I'd carried for so long began to lift. My thoughts became clearer, my body less tense. For the first time in a while, I felt grounded in myself.

I finally understood the meaning behind the phrase "mother knows best." Trusting my intuition had guided me through some of the most uncertain days of my life. And now, it gave me strength to move forward and focus on what came next for Landon. Nothing and no one would stop me.

Just as I began to feel proud of the determination I had shown as a mother, it was time for Landon's two-year old checkup with his pediatrician. I'd been both eager and uneasy about the appointment, especially in light of his recent diagnosis.

During the visit, Landon received a routine physical exam and developmental screening. He was also scheduled for vaccinations, which I chose to decline. Shortly after, he recommended that I take Landon to a developmental specialist as if he had not heard my concerns for almost a year. The doctor was not concerned because he was under two, but now that he was over two, he had to follow protocol.

In that moment, I was overwhelmed with anger and frustration. I had put in so much effort, time and again, to express my concerns about the possibility of autism. Yet, every attempt was dismissed. It felt like he didn't care to listen until it aligned with textbook guidelines.

I couldn't fully express the rage that bubbled inside me, but instead of engaging in an argument, I calmly asked for Landon's records to be released—we were leaving the practice to seek better care elsewhere. Even though I questioned whether attending the appointment was the right decision, I went through with it to speak directly about Landon's recent diagnosis and voice my disappointment.

Before leaving, I made one thing clear: *"Real-life experience can't be learned from books, and maybe you'll reconsider how you approach patient care."* I hoped my words stayed with him—that they would help prevent other families from enduring the same struggle we had.

In contrast, his new pediatrician showed a much deeper level of understanding and attentiveness. She recommended a re-evaluation of occupational therapy and an increase in speech services. Following the reassessment, Landon qualified for occupational therapy, expanded speech sessions, and continued developmental interventions through age three. However, a shortage of available therapists delayed the start of services. He was only able to receive a few weeks of occupational therapy before the school district assumed responsibility for his treatment.

When Eyes Overlooked, I Saw Him Clearly

From the moment Landon was born, I felt a connection to him that went beyond the typical parent-child bond. I noticed his unique quirks and sensitivities early on—an intuitive awareness that something set him apart. Even before the diagnosis, I sensed that he experienced the world differently, and I wanted to be the one to help him navigate it.

When we finally received the neurologist's confirmation, I was not surprised. I threw myself into learning everything I could, trying to anticipate the challenges ahead. I turned to every resource I could find—online communities, YouTube videos, books, articles, medical journals, and special education manuals—hoping that preparation would make the path forward a little easier.

But the most meaningful lessons came from Landon himself. The way he communicated, however fragmented or quiet, taught me more about his challenges, strengths, and the impact of autism on him than any expert could. Simple, everyday moments—things most people might overlook—revealed the depth of his spirit.

When I first realized that the nickname I gave him—"my little birdie"—would be tied to this lifelong journey, I was caught off guard. This experience has shaped how I see my son, reminding me to value the small victories that often go unnoticed.

Each milestone he reached struck a deep chord within me. The moment he spoke his first words again felt like music. Watching him throw a ball, instead of banging it, sparked joy in my heart. The day he tied his shoes or used the potty on his own felt monumental—like watching him climb a mountain. These moments filled me with pride and reassured me that he would be okay.

As I learned more about autism, I came to embrace it not as a limitation but as a vital part of Landon. Autism has become a thread in the fabric of our daily lives, bringing both challenges and immeasurable beauty. His unique lens on the world expanded my own. In celebrating his differences, I discovered a love deeper than I ever thought possible.

Helping Landon grow has helped me grow, too. I've developed extreme patience, compassion, and learned what it truly means to love without conditions. Supporting him isn't just about checking developmental boxes—it's about creating a life where he feels safe, accepted, and valued for exactly who he is.

Before Landon took his first breath, a fire lit within me—a devotion that only grew stronger when he entered the world. I became the embodiment of a protective mama bear, determined to shield him while also nurturing his kindness, his honesty, and the natural compassion he shows others. Every day, I strive to raise a boy who knows he is loved, seen, understood, and free to be his whole, beautiful self.

I'm prepared to do whatever it takes to ensure that Landon receives the same level of care and support he so freely gives to others. My commitment to him is steadfast— I will advocate for his needs and rights at every opportunity.

Whether it means navigating complicated systems, confronting unfair treatment, fighting for accommodations, or simply being his voice in difficult moments, I am determined to make sure he is treated with the respect and dignity he deserves.

CHAPTER *2*

Autism–His Unique Way of Life

From Uncertainty to Possibility

The early signs for my son were encouraging—he met his developmental milestones with bright-eyed excitement. From the moment he first crawled to the jumbled mix of sounds that became his first words, every achievement was a celebration. His laughter filled our home, and his curiosity was boundless.

The sight of birds gliding across the sky, leaves dancing in the wind, rain and snow falling from the sky, or planes soaring overhead sparked his imagination. His eyes would light up as he pointed excitedly, eager to share his discoveries. Everything filled him with wonder. But as the seasons changed, so did Landon—subtly at first, then unmistakably.

At first, the concerns were quiet murmurs. Landon, once so full of chatter and amusement, withdrew into a world of silence and frustration. His once-steady eye contact and contagious smile faded, like a photograph left too long in the sun—its vibrant details slowly blurring. Each time I called his name, and he didn't respond, a pang of uncertainty gripped my heart. Was it something I did? My mind raced through a frantic list of possibilities.

The enthusiasm faded. His gaze drifted downward when we walked, his world shrinking to the ground beneath his feet. When I held him close and pointed out a plane in the sky, he leaned into me, quiet and still without the wide-eyed curiosity that once made his whole face glow. It broke my heart to see that spark dim.

As days turned into weeks, my worry deepened. Laughter became rare, replaced by a stillness that settled over him like a thick fog. Social gatherings turned into battlegrounds of confusion—where he once played freely, he now lingered on the sidelines, his interactions dwindling. The vibrancy in his world dimmed, and with it, a part of him seemed to retreat. I documented everything, searching for patterns in his regressions—was it the hum of a vacuum, the overlapping voices at a party, the new outfit I just bought him, the brightness of the light, or the sudden excitement in a crowded playroom? The answers felt just beyond my reach.

Afternoons once spent reading and practicing sight words became silent struggles. As I flipped through picture books, Landon would rock and hum softly, his mind seemingly tangled in a web of thoughts. I pointed to illustrations, encouraging him to repeat the words, but his slow, fragmented responses only deepened his frustration. The effortless connection we once shared now felt like a message in a bottle, drifting further out to sea, waiting to be found. I longed for his bright smile as he looked up at me after discovering a picture that caught his attention. But it had disappeared.

As he moved through daycare and school, the challenges only grew. He became a quiet and fearful observer, his longing to join evident in the flicker of his gaze, yet an invisible barrier kept him from stepping forward. His silence extended beyond me—to his teachers, his classmates—his world shrinking with each passing day. And with a heavy heart, I realized Landon wasn't just losing words. He was losing his ability to connect.

Determined to help, I set out to create a nurturing environment—one where patience replaced guesswork and choices became invitations rather than assumptions. Instead of anticipating his needs, I encouraged him to make decisions for himself. What began as a simple exercise of holding up different objects gradually turned into a playful exchange, where he would reach for his preferred item, even though I longed for him to point and speak the words.

"Do you want milk, water, or juice?" I would ask, my voice filled with encouragement. His little brow furrowed, deep in thought like—Dwayne "The Rock" Johnson contemplating his next move. I could almost see the gears turning in his mind, a flicker of excitement lighting up his face just before he made his choice. In those moments, a spark of joy warmed my heart—a sign of progress, even if it didn't unfold exactly as I had envisioned.

Music became our refuge. Landon's love for melodies ignited something within him, leading me to use music as a bridge to clearer communication and connection. We jammed out in the car, danced in the living room, and lost ourselves in the rhythm, singing along to the tunes that resonated with him. In those moments, he mimicked sounds with delight, his laughter echoing through the house. Playing the same song over and over became an endearing ritual— each repetition carrying a hidden moment of understanding.

Yet as he grew older, his repeated phrases often lacked comprehension. It was a bittersweet symphony— each echo a testament to his effort, yet a reminder of the distance still ahead. With patience, I guided him through small corrections, not as reprimands, but as shared opportunities to understand the nuances of connection. His words, however unclear, were never just noise; each one was a step in his journey of self-discovery.

Conversations became the heart of our interactions—from animated discussions about dinosaurs, trains, and TV shows to moments of frustration when deeper expression eluded him. He thrived when the topic ignited his passion, yet on quieter days, his silence spoke louder than words. I understood that knowledge is power, so I introduced him to new ideas, planting seeds of curiosity that I hoped would grow into a greater understanding of the world.

One afternoon, during a routine walk, Landon surprised me. We paused at our favorite park—where he loved the rhythmic motion of the swings, and I cherished the warmth of holding him close in between each push. Suddenly, he pointed toward the sky, his voice breaking through the crisp air.

"Mama!" he exclaimed, excitement shimmering in his tone.

I followed his gaze. Above us, a flock of birds soared in perfect unison, their wings cutting through the sky with effortless grace. Their melodic calls filled the air, a symphony of movement and sound. My heart swelled. For the first time in a long while, I saw the light return to his face. At that moment, I knew—he could still find beauty in the world.

Routine was the foundation of Landon's world. The predictability of each day gave him a sense of control, like a steady current guiding him forward. But when that rhythm was disrupted—like the day heavy snow canceled school—his distress erupted in ways he couldn't fully express. Overwhelmed by the sudden change, he would throw himself to the floor or bang his head against the wall, his frustration spilling out in a storm of emotion. Each outburst shattered me, not because I was frustrated, but because I knew he was struggling to make sense of what he felt inside.

Yet, even within these challenges, hope surfaced. As Landon grew, I witnessed remarkable transformations. The meltdowns that once seemed inevitable became less frequent, replaced by quiet resilience. Where once he spiraled at the slightest disruption, he now found ways to adapt, his confidence softening the sharp edges of unpredictability. I celebrated each milestone—no longer bracing for an explosion when plans changed, but marveling at his ability to navigate life's complexities.

When he was little, trains were his world. His room was a vibrant tribute to his passion—walls adorned with posters of Thomas the Tank Engine and his friends, colorful shelves lined with an ever-growing collection of miniature locomotives, and a Thomas the Tank Engine bed covered with a matching comforter, sheet, and pillow. He could recite every episode and name every character, his excitement bubbling over whenever someone mentioned his favorite show.

"Thomas is blue, Percy is green"—with a cheerful smile! he would exclaim, his eyes shining as if each train carried a piece of his heart.

We often visited the nearby train station, where Landon would watch in quiet fascination. From the safety of the car, his wide eyes followed the massive locomotives as they rumbled past. Though the loud sounds kept him at a distance, he found comfort in the rhythmic chug of the engines and the gentle whoosh of the cars gliding along the tracks.

One particular toy train was his constant companion, Thomas. Its wheels spun endlessly between his fingers or at eye level, a quiet source of comfort when the world felt overwhelming. Whenever uncertainty or frustration crept in, he would reach for it, tracing its smooth edges, letting its familiar shape ground him in moments of chaos.

There were times I imagined Landon growing up to be a train conductor—his passion ran that deep. I could picture him in a crisp uniform, announcing destinations with confidence, guiding passengers on their journeys. But as he immersed himself in the world of trains, his curiosity expanded, branching into unexpected interests. Over the years, he discovered the joy of bowling, the excitement of WWE, the creativity of cooking and drawing, and the camaraderie of playing board games, Rummy 500, Fruit Ninja, and Family Feud with friends and family.

His curiosity burned bright, an unquenchable fire that drove him to dive wholeheartedly into each new passion. When something caught his interest, he absorbed every detail with astonishing focus. His ability to concentrate for long stretches, paired with his keen eye for detail, made him exceptionally gifted in whatever he pursued.

Landon also had a unique way of expressing his emotions. He often stimmed—flapping his hands, spinning, humming, or rocking movements that helped him process overwhelming and blissful moments. At first, understanding his cues was a learning experience, but over time, I became fluent in his unspoken language. Quick hand flaps signaled joy; slower, more deliberate motions hinted at sadness. If frustration took hold, a single head bang and a flop to the floor was often enough for him to release the tension and reset.

Spinning was his favorite. He would twirl with abandon, lost in the motion, his expression one of pure bliss. Each rotation seemed to lift him into another realm, a place where worries faded, leaving only joy. Watching him, I often felt dizzy, but my heart swelled with a happiness that consumed every part of me. Landon carried a light within—him—a beacon of innocence and wonder—that reminded me to embrace life's simplest, most beautiful moments.

As he twirled, his laughter rang out, bright and infectious. It wrapped around me, pulling me into his joy, and I couldn't help but smile. There was something mesmerizing about his ability to find happiness in the simplest motions—to spin himself into a world where nothing else mattered. Each dizzying whirl seemed effortless, as if he were dancing through his own universe, free and unburdened.

In the heart of our home, amid laughter and the gentle strumming of music, Landon found his voice—not just in spoken words, but in the connections, he learned to build. Through patience, empathy, and unwavering support, he transformed the silence that once separated him from others into a melody of communication uniquely his own, echoing the rhythm of a life embraced with promise.

Life moved at a pace that often overwhelmed him. Each day was an adventure filled with unpredictable challenges, testing his patience and adaptability. Sounds, textures, and sensations, whether at home, school, or outings—had the power to either soothe or unsettle him.

One morning, light streamed through his bedroom window, casting a soft glow as Landon stirred awake. He clung to familiar comforts, like his favorite fleece pajamas, the fabric's gentle embrace easing him into the day. But when it came time to get ready for the day, something was off. The soft cotton shirt I picked out—one he'd worn countless times before, suddenly felt unbearable against his skin. The khaki pants, usually a non-issue, became a source of distress. Without warning, frustration flared. He tugged at the fabric, his body tense, his eyes brimming with discomfort.

At first, I didn't understand what was wrong. But I knelt beside him, my voice calm as I asked, *"What's wrong, tell Mama? Are you tired? You want a hug?"* His body shook with silent sobs, his tears soaking into my chest as he clung to me. My heart clenched at his struggle.

Determined to ease his distress, I rubbed his back soothingly—but the tension remained. The growing discomfort intensified, making him feel increasingly agitated. I then changed his shirt, noticing how damp and clammy it was from his sweat and tears. Once I removed his shirt, a hesitant smile replaced his tears, though tension still lingered. I then swapped his pants for a softer pair, watching as relief washed over him. *"All betta,"* he murmured. As he hugged me, realization hit me like a ton of bricks—to pay close attention to his unspoken words and body language. And in that moment, I understood—sometimes, the smallest adjustments could change everything.

Landon had become attuned to textures. I noticed he often wore his socks inside out to avoid irritating seams. What seemed minor to others, was, to him, a necessary act of comfort. As he grew older, his preferences became more specific. He would only wear certain brands—Adidas, Under Armour, Champion, Tek Gear, or fleece—anything else was unbearable.

Loud noises, bright lights, and crowded spaces could easily overwhelm him. I remember our many attempts to take him to the movie theater—how his initial excitement would quickly give way to anxiety as the towering screen and booming speakers became too much to bear. The very place meant to create joy and wonder instead became a source of fear.

Relief came when I discovered sensory-friendly screenings, designed to create a gentler experience for kids like Landon. As he sank into the plush seat, the soft hum of the auditorium provided a soothing backdrop. The usual overwhelming elements were muted—the lights dimmed but not darkened, the volume lowered to a manageable level. I watched, awestruck, as his eyes lit up with pure excitement, fully immersed in the magic of storytelling on the big screen.

Seeing him so at ease in a space that had once unsettled him was a moment I will always cherish. It was a powerful reminder that the right environment could make all the difference.

Affection was his language. Landon loved to be held, hugged, and kissed, and I cherished the deep bond this created between us. Physical touch became his anchor, a way to find security in a world that often overwhelmed him. He would silently ask for a massage by lying on his stomach, and without hesitation, I would oblige, watching his body relax as my hands moved in soothing circles. The gentle pressure helped calm his nervous system, guiding him into a peaceful state.

Massages became an essential part of our daily routine, woven seamlessly into his world. Whether it was a quick rub on his head or feet, he sought that touch, especially on difficult days. I noticed his need for these moments of comfort increased when he was feeling particularly overstimulated.

At home, mealtimes brought their own challenges. Landon's diet revolved around crisp textures—chicken nuggets, crispy tacos, chips, French fries, toast, crackers, mac n' cheese, buttered pasta, cookies, and juice. I worried constantly, knowing his limited diet lacked the balance he needed. Any attempt to introduce something new—a soft fruit, a fresh vegetable, or a different protein—was met with resistance.

I watched helplessly as he recoiled from unfamiliar textures, gagging at yogurt, fruit, cucumber, baked chicken, Jello, Italian ice, or even milk. It wasn't always about taste; it was about the way certain foods felt in his mouth. Squishy, slimy, too cold, too hot, or soft textures triggered an instinctive rejection, deepening the divide between him and the variety I wished he could enjoy.

I wanted to help him expand his palate, to make mealtimes easier, but every failed attempt only reinforced his discomfort. And yet, despite the frustration, I never stopped hoping and trying.

Amid these struggles, there were moments of grace that made it all worthwhile. As night fell, we would settle onto the couch, eager to unwind after a long day. Landon would snuggle beside me under his favorite soft Thomas blanket, his beloved train clutched tightly in his hands as the world outside dimmed into quiet.

We'd turn on one of his favorite TV shows, The Wonder Pets, Thomas the Train, The Backyardigans, or sometimes embark on an adventure with Spider-Man or Toy Story. As the familiar sounds filled the room, I could see the tension melt from his body. He nestled closer, his small frame relaxing against mine, reassured by the warmth of my arm around his shoulders. As he began to feel sleepy, he crawled onto my lap, and I wrapped my arms around him, gently rubbing his head until he fell fast asleep. In those precious moments, the chaos of the day faded, replaced by the simple comfort of being together.

Sleep, however, was another challenge. The slightest sound or movement could wake him, pulling him from much-needed rest. To help him settle, our nightly routine became sacred—warm baths, soft pajamas, and the gentle scent of chamomile lotion as I massaged his skin. Occasionally, we used melatonin to ease him into sleep. Co-sleeping became the only way I could get a full night's rest because he felt safe—and I worried less. This ritual transformed bedtime into a sanctuary, a place where he could finally let go of the day's struggles and drift into peaceful rest.

Each challenge we faced together became an opportunity to understand his unique sensitivities. It was never just about giving in to his demands; it was about helping him navigate the world in a way that felt safe and comfortable. With every lesson, I learned to listen more deeply, to recognize that even the smallest discomforts held significance in his world.

As Landon grew, I watched him with a mix of sadness and admiration. He naturally gravitated toward solitary pastimes that allowed his creativity to flourish— drawing, completing puzzles, mazes, word searches, math problems, and hidden pictures. He preferred the steady rhythm of toy trains and the peaceful embrace of nature. There was beauty in the way he found comfort in his own world.

In the classroom, however, the lively atmosphere often felt overwhelming rather than inviting. Colors burst from the walls, bright posters filled the space, and the chatter of classmates swirled around him like a storm. It was too much. When the world outside became too loud, he retreated inward, where the vibrant hues dimmed, and voices faded into a distant hum.

Recess was no different. While other children ran, climbed, and shouted, Landon lingered at the playground's edge, seeking refuge in the steady motion of the swings. The rhythmic sway, the whispering leaves overhead—these small comforts helped him navigate a world that often moved too fast. In those moments, he could breathe.

Some saw his preference for solitude as a challenge to overcome, but I recognized it as a rare kind of self-assurance. He had built a relationship with himself that many struggle their whole lives to achieve. In his quiet world, he thrived. Though I sometimes wished for him to experience the joy of friendships that I — did — I also understood that solitude could be a teacher, for both of us. I admired the way he found joy in the smallest details—something I wished other children could see and appreciate. But I reminded myself that they, too, were on their own journeys of growth, each learning in their own way, just as Landon was.

Outside of school, children blended seamlessly into the joy of playground games, their laughter ringing through the air. But Landon often felt like an island, adrift in a sea of childhood energy. It was heartbreaking to watch him try to connect, only to struggle. His attempts at conversation sometimes came out as jumbled phrases, leaving his peers perplexed. More often than not, they walked away—faces clouded with confusion, indifference, or impatience.

Each time he stood on the sidelines, watching friendships unfold from a distance, I could see the unspoken question in his eyes: "Why is it so difficult for me to join in?" It wasn't just a game he was missing—it was the simple warmth of belonging.

Playtime for Landon was its own kind of adventure. While other children acted out elaborate stories with their toys, he found comfort in repetition, drawn to routines that brought him a sense of order. He would carefully line up his train cars, each one positioned with precise intention, forming a colorful, perfect sequence. Every morning, I would find him sitting in a W shape on the floor, spinning the wheels of his favorite engines at eye level, captivated by the rhythmic motion and the soft hum of their whirs. It was a small ritual, a moment of quiet delight that anchored him in a world that often felt unpredictable.

Sharing, however, was not so simple. His beloved engines were more than toys—they were a source of comfort, an extension of himself. His little fingers clutched it with quiet determination, his expression guarded whenever another child showed interest. I could sense the silent conflict in him—the desire to connect with his friends battling against the deep attachment he had to his trains.

Whenever a playmate reached for it, his body tensed, and in an instant, he would reclaim it, holding it close. It wasn't just possessiveness; it was security. Those small colorful engines had been with him through moments of excitement, frustration, fear, and change—they were a constant when the world felt overwhelming.

But over time, we helped him see that sharing didn't mean losing something—it meant gaining new experiences. I encouraged him to introduce his friends to his world of trains, to let them take part in the joy that filled him so completely. At first, he hesitated, reluctant to let go. But little by little, he softened. He began inviting them into his play, discovering the fun of racing trains along imaginary tracks and building bridges together instead of alone.

And then, one day, I saw it—the flicker of excitement in his eyes as laughter filled the room, not just his own but theirs, too. It was a small moment, but it was everything.

But when playtime didn't go as expected, expressing his feelings became a challenge. Frustration could lead him to rock back and forth, flap his hands, stiffen his body, or even throw himself onto the floor. If he wanted a toy someone else was playing with, he struggled to communicate his interest. Eventually, he learned to say, *"My turn."* However, he believed the words alone should immediately grant him access—which wasn't always the case. When using his words didn't get him what he wanted, he withdrew—frustration and sadness dimming the excitement that had once lit up his face.

Adults seemed to understand him better; their patience offered a safe space, free from the quick judgments of childhood and adolescence. He often remarked that grown-ups were kinder and slower to dismiss him. His heart longed for friendship, yet he was wise enough to recognize that not everyone sought meaningful connections.

Friendships were unpredictable and fleeting—like dandelion seeds carried off by the wind. Building connections didn't come easily to him, but Landon's journey was his own. He had learned to embrace who he was, cultivating a quiet yet unshakable companionship with himself. Perhaps, in time, he would find others who saw the world as he did—kindred spirits drawn together not by expectation, but by the unspoken understanding that the deepest connections often appear when we least expect them.

Landon is an only child, and I have always hoped he would have someone to share his life with, just in case his father or I were no longer around. While I knew he would have people looking out for him, it never felt the same. A deep, strong connection was missing until my nephew, whom I affectionately call "my little beast," was born in 2011. That day was a blessing as I witnessed my sister becoming a mother, myself becoming an aunt and godmother, and my son gaining a cousin—a lifelong best friend.

From the moment his cousin was born, they were inseparable. Landon's nurturing qualities shone through. At the sound of his cousin's cries, he would twirl his mobile above the bassinet, sing to him, show him his toys, feed him, or ask his mom to help. It was incredibly touching. As my nephew grew older, they became best friends.

Although they are years apart, I call my nephew "my little beast" because he embodies strength, toughness, and boldness. His fierce desire to protect his cousin is unstoppable, and his adventurous spirit encourages Landon to come out of his shell. The bond between my little birdie and my little beast is something I had only dreamed of, filling my heart with gratitude.

Despite their age difference and different personalities, they connected without question or judgment, embracing a friendship that I hope will last a lifetime.

Over time, I realized that every action—every focused moment, every twirl, every attempt at trying—was Landon's way of connecting with the world. His journey from an all-consuming love of trains to the many interests he explored was a testament to his boundless curiosity. Each day brought new discoveries, and I stood beside him, eager to see where his fascination would take him next.

Each morning, as we made our way to the bus stop, the sounds of the world grew louder around him. Honking horns, distant shouts, the rush of passing cars—all of it formed an invisible storm pressing in on him. Fear took hold, conjuring images of speeding vehicles, of unseen dangers lurking beyond the curb.

Seeking refuge, he would slip behind the sturdy trunk of a tree or press against my leg—or his dad's—using us as shields against the chaos of the outside world.

Repetition became our greatest ally. With time and consistent communication, a beautiful transformation began to unfold. He learned to trust that we would always ensure his safety. It wasn't a sudden leap but a gradual journey—a dance of trust that took steps toward independence.

One sunny morning, we decided it was time to test how far he had come. As we approached the bus stop, we exchanged a knowing glance. We gently stepped back, positioning ourselves a few meters away while still keeping a watchful eye on our brave little boy. At first, Landon hesitated, looking back at us with uncertainty. He would glance in our direction every few seconds to confirm we were still there, his safety net in this new role as the independent "big boy."

Each time he turned his gaze back to the street, ready to embrace the wait, we responded with encouraging thumbs-ups and warm smiles. *"Good job, big boy,"* we cheered, and with each bit of praise, Landon's confidence blossomed a little more. The fear that had once held him captive began to dissolve like morning mist under the rising sun.

Nearby, the laughter of children at the bus stop carried a bittersweet melody, one that tugged at Landon's heart. He longed to join their games, but anxiety held him back, its grip tightening whenever he thought about stepping forward. I saw the conflict in his eyes—the yearning to belong clashing with the fear that kept him on the sidelines. In those moments, I offered quiet encouragement, gently nudging him toward connection. But I also understood that, for him, the chaos of the world was not so easily tuned out.

Not every morning was a struggle. Some days, Landon's excitement was so radiant, I swore his smile could outshine the sun. Those were the moments I treasured most—the ones where he was free, unbothered, fully himself.

On those mornings, the world felt lighter, as if we were living inside a beautiful dream. Watching him embrace the day with joy filled me with gratitude, a reminder that happiness wasn't always out of reach. These glimpses of pure contentment painted our days with hope, and I held onto them, knowing there would be more—at home, at school, and beyond.

In discovering Landon's unique challenges, we found strength—often in the most unexpected places. His determination to succeed is nothing short of admirable, a quiet but unwavering force that inspires me every day. Time and again, he has pushed through doors I once feared would remain closed, revealing opportunities we had only dared to hope for. He reminded me that the beauty of life often lies in the simplest passions. In his eyes, ordinary moments became extraordinary, filled with creativity and spontaneity.

I've watched Landon confront obstacles that might have left others feeling defeated. Yet, he approaches them with a brave heart, his resilience shaping a definition of strength that extends beyond traditional measures of success. His journey is not just about achievement but about persistence, growth, and the courage to keep moving forward—even when the path ahead is uncertain.

Even when a door remains closed, I trust it will open when he is ready to step through. Our experiences have taught me that timing is everything. Progress doesn't always happen in a straight line, and while results may not be immediate, I have faith in his ability to navigate his own path. Each closed door is not a dead end but a pause—an opportunity for him to gather his skills and strength, self-reflect, and prepare for what lies ahead.

CHAPTER *3*

Navigating the Tide

Embracing Vulnerability in Motherhood

As a mother, I always wanted the best for my child, Landon. Yet, there were moments when I doubted whether I was enough. We had reached a critical juncture—it was clear that Landon's development lagged behind his peers. His speech was limited, and he often withdrew into his own world, missing social cues and milestones that other children navigated with ease.

People often portray the early days of motherhood in warm tones of joy and anticipation, but for me, an undercurrent of worry had been present from the moment my son was born. Landon, my vibrant son, moved through the world with a unique rhythm—captivating yet perplexing to those who encountered him. Despite my persistent concerns and careful observations, his doctor repeatedly assured me that nothing was wrong, leaving me alone with my spiraling fears.

It all began with a mixture of confusion and curiosity. I watched as Landon moved his hands in sweeping gestures, as if illustrating the flight of a bird. Those motions carried a deep, wordless meaning. Uncertainty drove me to seek answers. I spent my evenings absorbed in articles about autism, a topic I had stumbled upon unexpectedly.

The more I read, the more convinced I became that Landon's behaviors were not just childhood quirks but signs of something deeper. His frequent meltdowns, intense focus on specific toys, self-soothing behaviors, incoherent and fragmented speech, aversion to certain sounds, textures, and places, and tendency to withdraw or become extremely clingy all pointed toward autism. Each sign I recognized came with a chilling fear settling over me—one I hadn't allowed myself to fully acknowledge until that moment: my son might be on the autism spectrum, and we needed help now.

Confronted with this reality, my world felt unsteady, teetering on the edge of profound change. Many families found themselves trapped in the same frustrating struggle: an endless wait for therapy services that never seemed to move forward. The long waitlists loomed like dark clouds, casting shadows over the hopes of parents desperately seeking meaningful help for their children. My family was among them, navigating a labyrinth of challenges in our search for the right support for Landon.

Each day unfolded with a mix of urgency and determination. After learning that we did not need a referral to secure a specialist or treatment, the pressure of finding a therapist often led me to make hasty decisions. I would select the first available name on the list without fully vetting their qualifications or assessing whether they were the right fit for Landon's unique needs. It was a gamble driven by desperation—watching my son struggle left me feeling like I had no other choice.

But as I learned the hard way, availability didn't always mean suitability. Too many times, I sat in a therapist's office or observed from a window, watching as Landon struggled to connect, realizing that the wrong match only deepened his frustrations—and mine.

The road was difficult, especially with so few qualified professionals available. Still, we pressed on, working with the therapists we could find. I convinced myself that some support, however imperfect, was better than none. It wasn't easy to accept, but I held onto a sliver of hope that the right match would eventually come along. I clung to that hope because I knew it would take time—to explore, to understand Landon's needs, and to find the professionals who could truly help him.

With each therapy session, I saw small but meaningful progress. Every visit became an opportunity for Landon to build skills and confront his challenges head-on. He learned to articulate his feelings better, practiced social interactions, and took strides in recognizing his strengths. In those moments, I realized that even when a therapist wasn't the perfect fit, each session was still a step forward. I watched my son navigate the world one small victory at a time, a testament to his quiet resilience.

As we awaited the beginning of early intervention services, I believed that starting him in therapy early would be beneficial. The idea of receiving personalized attention and more frequent sessions felt promising. For the first time in a long while, I felt a sense of relief. Could this be the breakthrough we desperately needed?

At first, I hadn't even known early intervention services existed. For months, I had convinced myself that I had to handle everything alone, ignoring the toll it was taking on me. But as I read about the programs, I realized help was just a phone call away. I remember the moment I dialed the number—my heart pounded with a mix of anxiety and anticipation. After a thorough assessment, I learned that

Landon might qualify for additional services designed to support children like him.

Yet, uncertainty gripped me. What if he didn't qualify? The thought sent a wave of fear through me. If he was denied, our journey would become even more challenging. His doctor's repeated dismissal of my concerns only deepened my doubt and frustration. If a medical professional wouldn't acknowledge the struggles I saw every day, what hope did I have with early intervention? I questioned everything, wrestling with the fear that I might never find the support he so desperately needed. The road ahead felt like an endless maze—one I wasn't sure how to escape.

On the day of Landon's evaluation, I felt a mix of anxiety and hope. The specialist greeted us with a warm smile, immediately putting both Landon and me at ease. For nearly two hours, she assessed his development across multiple areas: communication, cognitive skills, self-help, social-emotional growth, and physical abilities. I watched as Landon engaged—hesitant at first but gradually opening up. Every response felt like a small victory, each sound a reason to press on, every smile a quiet sign of his willingness to try again.

Before the appointment, I had carefully prepared a detailed case summary, documenting my observations, concerns, and relevant medical records. This preparation proved invaluable, allowing me to present a clear picture of Landon's behaviors and bring attention to issues that might not have been immediately apparent. I wanted to ensure nothing was overlooked.

When the specialist confirmed Landon's eligibility for additional support, a wave of relief washed over me, bringing a smile that felt almost out of place amid my swirling emotions. But that relief quickly gave way to frustration—I had fought so hard for this moment, only to learn he qualified for speech therapy and nothing more. What was I seeing that no one else seemed to? I questioned myself. Were others truly blind to his struggles, or did they simply not care because he wasn't their child? I knew the road ahead would be difficult, but did it have to be this hard?

Although I was eager to see Landon thrive, the limited services available made my fight for more support feel endless. Each denial deepened both my determination and my despair. It felt like a battle I had to fight alone, one that weighed heavily on my heart. The specialist explained that I could appeal the decision or request another assessment if I disagreed. But for now, our focus had to be on developing his speech therapy plan through an Individualized Family Service Plan (IFSP) —a crucial step in laying the foundation for his developmental support.

The IFSP would identify Landon's specific needs, establish measurable goals, and outline the services that could help him progress. As we sat in our living room, I listened intently as the service coordinator explained the details. The plan not only documented Landon's developmental delays but also highlighted his strengths—his bright smile, infectious laughter, his curiosity, his willingness to try, and love for exploring pictures, shapes, sounds, and textures. She noted his deep interest in trains and music and how it could play a key role in supporting his development.

The plan was comprehensive, outlining targeted interventions tailored to Landon's unique needs alongside a structured treatment strategy designed to support his cognitive, social, emotional, and physical growth. While the primary focus was on speech, the service coordinator also suggested ways to help him progress in other areas where he fell within the expected developmental range.

The planning process gave me the opportunity to speak up, and I did. I asked about specific therapies, their objectives, and how they could be reinforced at home and in the places we explored together. The service coordinator listened patiently, answering my questions with empathy and understanding. She explained how various therapies—from speech to occupational therapy—could strengthen Landon's communication skills and fine motor abilities. Although I already had Landon enrolled in services and was knowledgeable of the pros and cons, I never disclosed this because I feared they would deny additional support.

Sensing my mixed emotions, she offered a gentle reassurance. *"Give him time to come around."*

I met her gaze, my voice firm. *"I've waited long enough, and I will do everything in my power to ensure no more time is wasted."*

I politely acknowledged her expertise as an early intervention coordinator, but as his mother, I had an intimate understanding of his needs. Something in my conviction must have resonated with her—her expression shifted, as if she suddenly saw my struggle in a different light. Concern flickered in her eyes, but I wasn't sure whether it was for me or the battle I was about to face.

Before leaving, she gently brought up a subject I hadn't considered. *"How are you doing with of all of this? It's important to acknowledge not just Landon's needs, but yours as well,"* she said, her voice warm and reassuring.

"This journey can be overwhelming, and it's okay to seek support for yourself."

My breath caught as I absorbed her words. Until that moment, I had been so focused on meeting Landon's needs that I hadn't paused to consider my own well-being. Overwhelmed by her kindness, tears stung my eyes. Having someone recognize my struggles and express genuine concern was unexpectedly moving.

She handed me information on parental support groups and online forums where I could connect with others facing similar challenges. She also recommended local counseling services specializing in family dynamics, reinforcing the idea that seeking help wasn't a sign of weakness, but a courageous step toward resilience—one that would ultimately help me be a stronger support for Landon.

As I listened, emotions surged, and I struggled to find the right words. *"I never realized… I mean, I was so focused on Landon and what he needed that I didn't even think about myself."* I exhaled, my voice carrying a mix of vulnerability and gratitude. *"Thank you for considering me in this process. He is my priority and as long as I'm breathing, I'll keep fighting."*

The service coordinator offered a gentle smile, her understanding evident. *"You're a vital part of his journey,*

Erica. Supporting Landon means taking care of yourself, too. Remember, you can't pour from an empty cup."

Her words struck a chord and quickly became my mantra, reminding me that prioritizing my well-being wasn't selfish—it was essential. If I wanted to remain strong and focused for Landon, I had to take care of myself, too.

Determined to find balance, I made a conscious effort to prioritize self-care. In the moment, I felt fine, but I knew it was only a matter of time before the weight of motherhood and this new reality took its toll. I joined support groups focused on autism, early intervention, special needs parenting, mental health, and women's empowerment. Expanding my support system beyond my immediate circumstances gave me a fresh perspective and a much-needed emotional reset.

I also rediscovered simple joys that had once been part of me. I experimented with new recipes in the kitchen, reorganized my home, wrote poetry, lost myself in romance and thriller novels, and cherished moments with friends. I treated myself to nail salon visits, indulged in facials and massages, and committed to regular workouts with my sister and best friend. Each activity provided a sense of balance, allowing me to nurture myself while still being fully present for Landon.

Engaging in these activities helped me reconnect with who I was outside of being a mother. They became a refuge from the emotions I hadn't fully processed—the quiet grief over how different motherhood looked from what I had imagined. I hadn't realized how much of myself I had lost until I started reclaiming the pieces.

As I processed my emotions, I often felt an intense sadness, quickly followed by overwhelming gratitude for my baby boy. I thought of women who longed for children but might never have them, and in that instant, my heart swelled with appreciation for the gift of motherhood. Though my experience looked different from what I had imagined—filled with unexpected challenges—I reminded myself to cherish it, knowing how fragile and precious it truly was. My heart ached, and still aches, for those who may never know this joy.

During moments of self-care, clarity emerged. Instead of dwelling on what was missing, I focused on the many blessings God had given me. There were—and still are—days when uncertainty weighs on me when I ruminate about the difficulties ahead. But I choose gratitude, seeing each challenge not as a roadblock but as an opportunity for growth.

I often wished I could take away all of Landon's struggles, to carry them myself, and accepting that I couldn't was a heavy burden. Yet, taking care of myself made me stronger. I saw that through all the doctor's appointments, therapy sessions, and sleepless nights, I was still standing— still fighting, still adapting. And in that, I found moments of empowerment.

This journey ignited a deep resolve within me—to understand my son's world, to grasp how autism shaped his emotions, his learning, and his place in an often-overwhelming environment. Though he had not yet received a formal diagnosis, I embraced the reality of his condition to better support him. I became his voice, his advocate, speaking up when he could not. Deep down, I clung to the hope that one day, someone would truly listen.

That day finally arrived just after his second birthday. When Landon's diagnosis was confirmed, a flood of emotions overtook me—relief, gratitude, fear, uncertainty, anger, and a profound sadness. It felt as though I were carrying the weight of both his diagnosis and my own helplessness.

Yet, as we stepped into this new reality, clarity slowly took hold. Amidst the emotional storm, I realized that every challenge, every unanswered question, had led us here.

This wasn't just a diagnosis; it was a doorway to deeper understanding. It marked a turning point—a shift in perspective. I began to see every small step as progress, every moment of connection as a victory.

My mission evolved. I sought and secured new ways to support Landon as he navigated an unpredictable world. I celebrated the little milestones—the extra second of eye contact, the moments he truly engaged in play, the times he imitated actions without prompting, his courage in wearing unsuitable clothing to a special event. Each was monumental, a reminder that he was moving forward in his own way, on his own terms.

Through this perspective, I found hope. I recognized that each challenge was also an opportunity for learning and connection. I played with Landon, observing his preferences and how they helped him flourish. I read books, attended workshops and therapy trials, and consulted specialists who offered insights into strategies tailored to his needs. Along the way, I discovered a community of parents with similar experiences. Together, we built a support system where we could lean on one another, sharing resources, celebrating victories, and navigating moments of vulnerability.

With every conversation and each new piece of knowledge, I felt more prepared to help Landon navigate his world with confidence. He was often anxious about speaking to his peers, so I encouraged him to start with a simple greeting and a smile. Over time, this small action became a bridge, easing his fears and inviting others into conversation. The joy he felt when he was acknowledged eased his anxiety about rejection, and seeing his confidence grow filled me with pride. He was learning, just as I was, that progress—no matter how gradual—led to meaningful change.

As I held Landon's hand through this journey, I realized my fears weren't meant to paralyze me but to push me forward. With each passing day, I grew to appreciate his unique personality, celebrating his curiosity, strengths, and potential as we adventured together. My resolve only deepened.

I was no longer just an observer in his world—I was his advocate. I immersed myself in exploring new methods that would allow him to express himself and learn in ways that made sense to him. I sifted through different therapeutic approaches—weighted blankets, salt caves, foot reflexology—as well as educational techniques like writing tools, flashcards, and asking questions after each story paragraph he read to enhance his comprehension—determined to find what truly resonated with him.

I had become disillusioned with conventional therapy that focused on age-appropriate milestones. I yearned for a more organic approach that allowed him to flourish uniquely. When he expressed himself freely, his true essence—creativity, joy, and spontaneity—emerged. I wanted to nurture our bond and encourage him to explore his interests at his own pace, free from societal pressures.

I discovered that Landon thrived in environments where he could engage his senses—sensory play became our new favorite pastime. Together, we filled bins with rice, sand, beans, water, and colorful toys, letting him run his fingers through the textures, watching as he lost himself in the colors and sensations. The pure delight on his face as he explored each new feeling filled my heart with warmth.

Communication tools became a cornerstone of our routine. With guidance from therapists, we introduced picture exchange systems and simple sign language to help Landon express his needs and emotions. Watching a few images and finger movements unlock a world of connection between us was nothing short of magical. The frustration of silence slowly faded, replaced by moments of understanding and shared expression.

As we ventured down this path, I found solace in embracing the imperfections. Some days, progress felt stagnant; setbacks made me question everything. But instead of letting those moments consume me, I accepted them as part of the process. They reminded me that growth wasn't linear and that every challenge was an opportunity to reassess and adapt.

Landon's laughter became a melody I cherished, its significance deepening as I learned to appreciate the simplicity and beauty of his expressions. The more time I spent engaging with him, the more I understood how he saw the world—a vibrant, ever-shifting landscape of wonder.

Watching him play was a reminder of my own childhood and how beautiful simple moments could be. As he buried his toy trains in the rice, I could see his mind at work, crafting stories and adventures only he could imagine. These small acts of play became his language, a way of expressing himself and finding joy in his own space. Gratitude washed over me as I realized he was thriving in his own unique way.

"You are perfect," I whispered, hoping the sincerity of my words reached him. A reply wasn't necessary. I only needed him to hear my heart, even if he didn't fully understand.

Each day brought opportunities for growth—not just for Landon, but for me as well. The challenges that once felt overwhelming gradually became pathways to deeper understanding. I saw the world through his eyes—a place brimming with unconditional love, wonder, curiosity, and unexpected intricacies. He was ensuring that the world worked in his favor, rather than against him.

While uncertainty may always linger, I've come to realize it does not define us. Instead, security, understanding, acceptance, and unwavering love guide our path forward. There is a quiet strength within our family, sustained by the perseverance we've shown in the face of adversity.

Landon, in his own way, has taught me the beauty of patience and the profound importance of communicating beyond words. Through his actions, his expressions, and his moments of connection, I've learned to appreciate the subtle nuances of our relationship. I understand now that setbacks do not mean failure—true failure only happens when we stop trying. Limited resources and rejection made this lesson clear to me early on.

A weight lifted off my shoulders as I reflected on how far we had come—how much we had endured without breaking. I realized I could embrace our new life without guilt. For the first time, I truly enjoyed my moments of self-care, rather than just going through the motions. Whether reading a novel, listening to my favorite podcasts, or soaking in the calmness of a salt cave infused with essential oils, I used this time to recharge, honoring my body and mind with the care they deserved.

Prioritizing my well-being allowed me to absorb new research relevant to Landon's journey. With a clearer mind, I could process information, make informed decisions, and move forward with confidence. I could finally breathe easier, reassured that everything would be okay. Embracing my roles as both a mother and an advocate empowered me, clarifying my identity and strengthening my sense of purpose.

Receiving a formal diagnosis took more than a year and assembling the right team of professionals took even longer. The process felt like an endless cycle of meetings, evaluations, and consultations—each one bringing a mixture of hope and frustration. It often felt like navigating a maze, searching for the right path but finding myself lost in a tangle of conflicting opinions.

Yet, as I immersed myself in understanding my son, I realized that truly supporting him required more than expert advice—it required trusting my own instincts. I spent countless hours observing him, noting his unique strengths and challenges, and feeling the ebb and flow of his emotions. In those quiet moments of reflection, I discovered the power of acceptance, perseverance, and courage. These qualities mattered far more than the fear of judgment, the weight of doubt, or the temptation to deny reality.

Each day, I learned to celebrate small wins only I could see—the sparkle in his eyes when he solved a math problem, recognized a word, expressed his thoughts, helped someone, earned an accolade, completed a household chore without help, made a new friend, or practiced his favorite sport, bowling, with unwavering determination. These moments unveiled his true spirit and steadfast work ethic. I cherished how he navigated the world in his own unique way, a perspective often overlooked by those who focused only on his challenges.

This mindset shift enabled me to guide him in ways that truly met his needs. I no longer sought validation from professionals or worried about outside opinions. My only priority was doing what was best for my son. Shortly thereafter, he began to celebrate his victories, beaming with pride every time he accomplished something he had previously found difficult.

When he played baseball and basketball for the first time, getting a hit or making a basket wasn't just a win for him; it meant everything. Even while the game was still ongoing, he would look for me, offering a smile or clapping his hands. Sometimes, he ran off the field or court just to receive a hug, and I welcomed him with open arms. Ensuring he felt supported—never defined by his challenges—became essential during these moments.

With time, my role as his advocate evolved. While I remained by his side, I also encouraged him to build the confidence and skills to speak up for himself. Self-advocacy became a central focus as he grew. I urged him to express his thoughts and needs openly, to communicate with family, peers, doctors, and educators without guilt or hesitation.

Whether he would eventually navigate this independently or with minimal support, my priority was instilling in him a sense of agency and self-assurance. I envisioned a future where he moved through the world not weighed down by fear or doubt but empowered by the understanding that his voice mattered as much as anyone else's.

Had I ignored my instincts, I might have missed crucial opportunities for my son's growth. The thought lingers—I often wonder where he'd be today had I silenced my concerns or accepted outside opinions. But I remind myself that trusting my instincts wasn't just protection; it was love in action. The uncertainty of our journey was daunting, yet that very uncertainty fueled my determination to seek the support he needed.

Every decision felt like a heavy weight on my heart as I navigated the countless options before me. I knew each choice could shape his future, and that knowledge solidified my belief: acting early would give him the strongest foundation to learn, grow, and thrive. Standing still wasn't an option while the world kept moving. I realized my choices would either strengthen him or leave him exposed.

In those early days, every appointment and consultation felt like a step into the unknown. I was an explorer venturing into uncharted territory, guided only by my instincts and an unwavering love for my son. Doubts crept in, making me question my efforts, but each time uncertainty took hold, I returned to what I knew—his laughter, his moments of insight, his unique way of seeing the world. These reminders fueled every choice I made.

It wasn't just about obtaining a diagnosis; it was about identifying the resources and support he needed to thrive. The journey was filled with unexpected twists— moments of triumph woven together with challenges. Yet, each hurdle revealed strengths in him I hadn't anticipated. His empathy and compassion for others, even in the face of unkindness, was remarkable. He developed a sharp eye for overlooked details, respected others' boundaries without question and care, and remained steadfastly true to himself.

Had I let fear dictate my choices, I might have missed the quiet yet profound transformations—how he learned to set goals, adapt to his environment, build friendships, and advocate for himself.

As I reflect on the many diagnoses and medical conditions Landon has received over the years, I recognize the importance of honoring his unique experiences. Each diagnosis isn't merely a label but a meaningful chapter in his story—one that captures his strengths, struggles, and daily triumphs. To overlook these defining experiences would diminish the depth of his journey—a journey marked by resilience, growth, and invaluable lessons worth sharing.

These names and categories serve as tools for understanding, not limitations. They have offered us insights that help us navigate the complexities of his world, but they do not define it. Landon is so much more than any diagnosis. He is a vibrant individual, a young man with a passion for becoming a chef, dreams of going pro in the PBA, and a perspective that enriches the lives of those around him.

Sharing our journey feels vital because it reflects the experiences of so many others—past, present, and future. Autism is not a one-size-fits-all experience. As Dr. Stephen

Shore wisely said, "If you've met one person with autism, you've met one person with autism." This truth resonates deeply with me, underscoring the individuality of every person on the spectrum. Each person is unique, shaped by distinct personalities, strengths, challenges, and experiences. Their paths are influenced not only by their characteristics but also by the support systems around them, the understanding of their families, and the resources available in their communities.

Landon's story is one of hope and possibility, a testament to the power of perseverance. It reminds me that while obtaining a diagnosis can provide guidance and access to support, it should never overshadow the essence of a person.

I know how easy it is to feel discouraged, to undervalue the small but significant progress being made. I understand how fear can hold you back when all you want to do is move forward. I know how not being heard makes you want to crawl into a hole and give up. I know how anger can eclipse all the good things in your life. I know how easy it is to get lost in trying to help someone you love. I've been that parent, trapped in a world that I didn't feel was my own—a time I don't regret.

For me, fully embracing my role as Landon's mother meant offering him unwavering love and support while also recognizing when to step back. Each day was a delicate balance—guiding him through life's challenges while understanding that sometimes, the most powerful act was giving him the space to find his own way.

There were moments when my instincts urged me to intervene—to offer help or solutions. The weight of my responsibility pressed heavily—I wanted to shield him from difficulties. Yet, each time I paused and stepped back; I witnessed something profound. I saw him rise to the occasion, navigating his own path with a determination that took my breath away. He thrived when given the chance to make choices, take risks, and learn from his experiences. Allowing him to explore and grow on his own terms became essential—not only for his development but for the strength of our relationship.

Yet, as I taught my son, he taught me. Without words, he imparted wisdom that deepened my trust in my instincts as a mother. Each day became a lesson in empathy, patience, and love. I learned to let go of preconceived expectations and focus on his true needs and desires rather than what I assumed should happen. He has changed my outlook on many things. My values and beliefs are clearer now, and I appreciate the beauty in life I had overlooked before. It is a humbling process—one that challenged me to redefine my understanding of unconditional love, strength, success, progress, and more.

When faced with uncertainty—those moments heavy with questions and doubt—I lean into it instead of allowing outside voices to dictate my choices. That's when the world's whispers of doubt grow quieter, replaced by a steady confidence in my voice as a parent. I have found strength in accepting that I don't have all the answers and recognizing when I need to ask for help, a lesson that continues to guide me today. With Landon leading the way through his unique experiences, kind heart, warm presence, and contagious personality, I have gained a clearer perspective on navigating the unknown.

CHAPTER *4*

Unmasking Reality

Embracing What We Always Knew

I envied other parents who seemed to navigate parenting effortlessly and children who developed skills with ease. I wondered if they, too, juggled endless appointments, therapists, and case workers moving in and out of their homes, or if they carried unanswered questions. Did they lose sleep at night? Did they know what it was like to raise a child with special needs? Did they worry about their child's future after they were gone? Was their child displaying odd behaviors, regression, or delays? Did they have a doctor who listened?

My new reality brought emotions I had never experienced, and I struggled to understand why. It felt like grief. I wrestled with irrational fears of the unknown, guarded myself, and found it hard to trust others. Seeing the good in anything became difficult, and I longed for the life I once had. The storm of emotions and thoughts felt like an explosion that buried me, leaving me desperate for rescue. But I had to save myself—no one else could.

I remember sitting in the park, watching my son lie on the pavement, dragging his little red-and-yellow plastic bike at eye level across the basketball court. All I could think was how beautiful and unique he was. In that moment, I realized that envying others was pointless—what I saw on the surface might not reflect their reality. I didn't know their journeys well enough to assume their lives were perfect. Why was I convincing myself they had it better than I did?

A few moments later as my son ran toward the swings, calling for me to pick him up and push him, I smiled through tears of joy. I had been caught in a riptide, but my body had instinctively swum parallel. It felt like I had discovered a message in a bottle washed up on the shore—a rare and personal revelation meant just for me. I thought, *"Look at what you have in front of you—so innocent and happy. You have everything you ever dreamed of. Remember, Erica, he chose you."* Those quiet words echoed through me and saved me. In that moment, I knew I needed to find support to help me navigate this journey.

My family and friends were my support system, but I didn't want our time together to feel like a therapy session. I knew they would listen, or at least, I hoped, but I doubted they would truly understand what I was going through. Most didn't have children yet and those who did weren't experiencing motherhood the way I was. Looking back, I realize my inability to fully connect with them was my own doing. I never truly let them in.

Still, their presence helped me reclaim my sense of self, and it felt good. Even though I didn't open up, simply having them around was what I needed. I craved moments where I could just be myself—to laugh, to reminisce, to escape the worries that weighed on me daily. I cherished our time together, especially our "one tree hill nights." The most comforting part was that no matter what was happening with Landon, they never pointed it out. They embraced him completely and seeing that meant the world to me. I will always be grateful for their support.

Before I discovered support groups, journaling was my escape. Writing gave me a space to express my thoughts freely and process my emotions without fear of judgment. It wasn't that I was hiding my feelings—I just didn't want my sadness to become a burden for others. Through my daily entries, I reminded myself to stop comparing my life, my son, and myself to others, knowing that what I saw on the surface was never the full story.

I learned to shift my mindset from dwelling on the negatives to recognizing the positives through self-reflection. Rather than envying others because that wasn't the person I wanted to be—I made it a daily practice to appreciate what I had and work toward what I didn't. While waiting for his neurologist appointment, I came to understand the power of self-compassion in navigating life's unexpected changes.

The day of our visit to the pediatric neurologist arrived in a whirlwind of emotions—a mix of anxiety and guarded optimism churned within me. As I sat in the waiting room, watching other families carry their own burdens, a heaviness settled in my chest. This was the moment we had been waiting for, yet it felt like we had already run a marathon just to get here.

It took forever to reach this point, I thought, glancing at my son as he busied himself with the toys in the play area. His innocent smile sparked a flicker of hope in the midst of my tangled thoughts, but guilt quickly followed. We should have been here sooner. The signs had been there—soft whispers that went unheard.

Reflecting on our journey, I felt weighed down by the countless unproductive doctor visits, the limited support from early intervention services, the ignorant stares and comments, and the sheer amount of time it had taken to reach this point. I blamed myself for not being able to articulate my son's struggles—how could I put into words the moments when he seemed lost in his own world, the way he stared at walls as if searching for answers? I blamed myself for wasting precious time, for not being the advocate he needed.

Then, my frustration turned to his pediatrician—a doctor I had once trusted but now saw in a different light. I blamed him for not being transparent, for failing to guide us in the right direction, and for not listening. When had he missed the signs? Why hadn't he pushed for answers when I needed them most? It was maddening to realize how trust could erode, leaving only frustration in its wake.

The weight of these emotions pressed down on me daily, but here I was, finally in the right place, staring at the door that held the possibility of answers—or at least, I hoped. I closed my eyes for a moment, drawing in a deep breath. When I opened them again, I looked at my son. His playful voice filled the room, and for the first time in weeks, I felt like I could breathe again.

The nurse called us in, and my heart pounded as we stepped into the small, brightly lit room lined with charts and anatomical models. Moments later, the neurologist entered, her calm demeanor and warm smile both inviting and reassuring. She introduced herself with a quiet confidence that immediately eased some of my fears. As she explained what to expect during the appointment, her voice carried a steadiness that felt like an anchor in the storm of my emotions.

Each word was a fragment of clarity in a world that had felt foggy for far too long. I leaned in, hanging onto every detail as she spoke. She asked thoughtful questions, listening intently without rushing. My defenses began to lower—this wasn't the conversation I had feared, one filled with dismissiveness, blame and uncertainty. Instead, it was one of understanding and possibility.

When she turned her attention to Landon, I watched as she engaged with him in a way that felt effortless and genuine. She knelt to his level, meeting his eyes with warmth, making him feel seen and valued. She didn't just see a diagnosis—she saw a child full of potential. The way she patiently mirrored his playfulness sparked something within me, a small but powerful sense of hope and connection.

I observed as she carefully noted his reactions—how he explored the toys, how curiosity flickered in his eyes, and even the moments when he self-soothed and withdrew. This was more than a clinical assessment; it was a sincere effort to understand who Landon was as a person. Her dedication to truly seeing him made me trust the process, filled me with renewed hope, and allowed me to slowly let my guard down again.

Landon's appointment involved a series of tests designed to uncover any underlying challenges. As we moved through each evaluation, I could sense his mild anxiety, yet I was struck by his resilience. Despite the unfamiliar setting and the weight of the moment, he approached each task with a mix of curiosity and determination. Watching him, I felt something shift within me—recognition of the strength I had always known was there.

After what felt like an eternity of assessments, we finally received the diagnosis: Pervasive Developmental Disorder–Not Otherwise Specified (PDD-NOS), accompanied by sensory processing challenges—just as I had suspected. The moment hung in the air, carrying relief and gravity. The clarity we had been searching for was finally within reach, although a small part of me wished I was mistaken. Tears flooded my eyes, but all I could do was smile, place my hand over my heart, and exhale.

Hearing the diagnosis triggered a flood of emotions. For so long, I had carried the weight of doubt and guilt, questioning my parenting and every decision I had made. Had I missed the signs? Am I imagining things? Could I have done something differently? The uncertainty had been exhausting, and as the neurologist confirmed what I had long suspected, I felt a release.

As she discussed Landon's case, she emphasized the importance of early advocacy and the role of dedicated parents in shaping their children's futures. Her encouragement reignited something in me, lifting my spirits after months of emotional and mental exhaustion. I had felt disconnected for so long, but in that moment, I began to reclaim my sense of self. Her sensitivity and guidance reminded me that we weren't alone—this was a journey we would navigate together, for Landon's sake.

As we scheduled our follow-up appointment and stepped out of the office, I held Landon's hand tightly, feeling a renewed commitment to advocating for him and ensuring he received the support he needed. This was the beginning of a new chapter and for the first time in a long while, I could see the road ahead with clarity.

This diagnosis wasn't just a label; it was a key to understanding Landon's unique way of experiencing the world. It provided answers and unlocked access to essential resources—speech therapy, occupational therapy, applied behavior analysis, coping strategies, and more. The doubt that had plagued me began to lift as I realized we could now move forward with purpose and support.

The neurologist's unwavering focus on Landon reassured me that he was more than a diagnosis—he was a child with potential, deserving of care beyond just medical terms. Gratitude swelled within me. The road ahead would have its challenges, but this moment felt like a turning point—a beacon of hope guiding us toward a future filled with understanding, acceptance, and growth.

We made plans for our next steps—therapies, routines, and activities that would allow Landon to explore his interests. I envisioned afternoons filled with art projects, science experiments, board games, and countless trips to the park and zoo, where he could engage with the world in his own way. I could already hear his laughter as he watched the monkeys swing from the trees at his favorite zoo.

In the weeks that followed, our lives found a new rhythm. Our days were filled with learning and exploration, and slowly but surely, I noticed changes in Landon. He became more engaged, more confident in sharing his ideas, less fearful, and each small milestone filled my heart with joy. We were making progress one day at a time.

During our next visit, the neurologist presented her comprehensive findings, seamlessly connecting insights from our discussions with results from follow-up tests. It was more than just an analysis—it was a blueprint of possibilities, reigniting my commitment to developing tailored activities that would enhance Landon's strengths and support his needs.

Together, we crafted strategies that nurtured both growth and resilience. I sought advice from specialists, pored over research, enrolled him in sports, and explored different therapies and classes, determined to find what would best empower him. I wholeheartedly believed that the combination of private therapy and early intervention paved the way for his success. Every new tool we discovered, every technique we implemented, became part of our growing toolkit, helping us face each day with optimism.

Challenges still arose, but they became stepping stones rather than roadblocks. I learned to celebrate the small victories—his ability to focus a little longer, his willingness to step outside his comfort zone, his attempt to try a new food, his attraction to other toys, and his excitement in sharing his thoughts with friends. Each moment reminded me of his incredible spirit and deep desire to connect with the world around him.

I built strong partnerships with Landon's doctors, teachers, therapists, and other parents, forming a network of advocates dedicated to ensuring the best possible future for our children. We exchanged ideas, shared strategies, and encouraged one another, creating a sense of community that made the journey feel less isolating. In this environment of teamwork and support, Landon flourished.

He began participating in group activities, learning to express himself, exploring various textures, problem-solving, and interacting with peers. I watched in awe as he took the initiative to join school clubs and sports, his confidence growing with each new experience. His opinions became something I cherished—a sign that he was finding his place in the world through his own observations and perspectives.

Each day felt like a win, reinforcing my belief that we were moving in the right direction. Together, we adapted. When challenges arose, we reevaluated the strategies, adjusted our approach, and continued moving forward.

What began as a journey filled with doubt, fear and uncertainty had transformed into a testament to hope, acceptance, connection, and determination. Landon and I grew closer, bound by love and perseverance, navigating the complexities of life hand in hand. My mission became clear: to ensure he never faced anything alone. Armed with a solid plan, we prepared for whatever lay ahead, staying informed on the latest autism research, treatments, and strategies to give him the best possible support.

Navigating the constant flow of information proved to be a rollercoaster of emotions for me. I found myself overwhelmed by the sheer volume of data, which fueled negative thoughts, fear, and a never-ending quest for answers. Yet, amidst these challenges, there were moments of inspiration that encouraged me to engage with the world in a more positive light.

After Landon's diagnosis in May 2009, our world shifted dramatically. We had become part of a growing community of families grappling with the rising prevalence of autism worldwide. As I immersed myself in research, I encountered startling statistics: the diagnosis rate had jumped from 1 in 110 children in 2009 to 1 in 88 the following year. By 2025, it had skyrocketed to 1 in 31. This rapid increase raised a storm of questions within me, sparking an unrelenting search for answers—not only on a global scale but also for our family.

Why were more children being diagnosed? Had I or someone else overlooked something? Was I a negligent parent? Had I done something wrong? Will my son regress? Will his future be affected? These questions haunted me, fueling my self-doubt. I sought clarity from professionals, but the answers were vague, leaving me more unsettled than before. Instead of finding certainty, I found myself drawn toward understanding Landon beyond his diagnosis. The focus felt too much on autism, not enough on the person, so I was determined to change that. My focus shifted inward as I wrestled with societal expectations, personal fears, and the evolving reality of our lives.

Our story intertwined with the experiences of countless other families navigating similar paths. I connected with a vast network of parents, each with their own struggles and triumphs. In meetings and online forums, I read and listened to their heartfelt accounts—stories of love, resilience, and frustration that mirrored my own. I found comfort in their words, realizing I wasn't the only parent facing such challenges.

I shared Landon's progress, just as they shared their children's successes. Yet, even with the support, a lingering sadness often crept in. Tears welled in my eyes—not just for Landon or myself, but for every parent taking their first steps down this uncertain road. I knew something needed to change, but I didn't know where to start. Each time I tried to envision a solution, my mind went blank, my heart heavy with exhaustion.

So, I wrote. I captured our journey towards a diagnosis, our daily routines, the small victories, new adventures, new words spoken, friendships made, milestones achieved, negative experiences, and the beautiful little quirks that made Landon unmistakably himself.

With every word, I found strength—not just for myself, but for others who might one day read our story. I chronicled the way his laughter erupted in bursts, how he could become completely immersed in his favorite toys, lost in a world only he could see, and how he exhibited compassion towards those who were unkind. I listed every new word he uttered or attempted, eagerly anticipating more to come. I described the moments of connection—those fleeting instances when he would lift his gaze from his play, his eyes shining with a recognition of joy that took my breath away. I observed his progress: the focused intensity with which he maneuvered the hula hoop, first from head to waist, until it finally fell, only to be replaced by a smile that deeply touched my heart.

By recording the positives in my journals and organizing the challenges in his medical binder, I found a way to separate reflection from strategy. This balance allowed me to celebrate his progress while ensuring he received the support he needed.

As I continued researching, I discovered an even broader spectrum of experiences among children like Landon. Some required ongoing, hands-on support, while others thrived with independence. The more I learned, the more I saw the beauty in these varied paths.

In my quest to better understand autism—and to steer my mind away from negative thoughts—I found myself drawn to the film Rain Man. With only a basic knowledge of the condition, I felt compelled to explore this widely discussed portrayal. I watched it repeatedly, absorbing every nuance, eager to gain insight into a world that felt both distant and deeply personal.

Pen in hand, I took notes, immersing myself in the story. With each viewing, new layers emerged. I studied how Raymond Babbitt navigated life, the idiosyncrasies that defined him, and the moments of connection he shared with his brother, Charlie. Their complex relationship captivated me—it mirrored the struggles and joys many families experience.

Emotions washed over me in waves. Some scenes made me laugh, while others brought unexpected tears and "aha" moments. I empathized with Raymond's struggles—his difficulty with social interactions, the overwhelming weight of sensory overload—yet I also admired his extraordinary abilities, like his astonishing memory and mathematical brilliance. Autism, I realized, wasn't a single experience but a vast spectrum of diverse stories.

One scene struck me with particular force: the chaos of the casino, where flashing lights and clattering sounds enveloped Raymond. The sensory overload felt suffocating, and as I watched, my thoughts turned to Landon. How would he navigate a world that often moved too fast, too loud, too unpredictably? A tightness formed in my chest as I imagined him in a similar situation—lost in the noise, overwhelmed, and afraid. And worst of all, what if I couldn't comfort him? What if, in his distress, he pushed me away? The weight of that fear pressed down on me, settling deep in my heart.

But amid that pain, something unexpected emerged. As I watched, I began to see the power of self-regulation—those small, soothing rituals that brought comfort amid chaos. I had never considered them in this way before. Raymond's ability to concentrate despite the overwhelming noise, to find solace in familiar patterns, revealed a different perspective. This depiction, though fictional, sparked something within me—a sense of hope. It shifted my focus from fear to possibility, urging me to reimagine what Landon could achieve rather than dwell on perceived limitations.

In those quiet moments of reflection, I realized that Landon's journey would unfold with its own unique rhythms, shaped by rituals and coping mechanisms that made sense to him. I began to see potential where I once saw uncertainty. Just like Raymond, Landon could develop his own ways of navigating the world, honing strategies to manage his sensory experiences.

Embracing this shift in perspective allowed me to rethink my role as his guide. Instead of fearing life's unpredictability, I focused on how I could help Landon recognize and develop his strengths. I envisioned creating a safe space at home—a place where he could explore his interests, build routines, and practice self-soothing techniques, free from judgement. Much like Raymond's moments of quiet concentration, these would become his anchors in a world that often felt overwhelming.

The more I embraced this understanding, the more empowered I felt. The world might resemble a noisy casino at times—full of distractions, flashing lights, and unexpected disruptions—but Landon and I could navigate it together. By honoring his unique way of experiencing life, I could nurture his self-awareness and help him thrive amid the noise.

In the end, Rain Man was more than a film. It became a lesson in empathy, understanding, acceptance, diversity, and the beauty of individual journeys. It reminded me that every child, including Landon, deserves the chance to flourish. With each passing day, I grew more determined to embrace the full spectrum of strengths and challenges that defined our lives.

After receiving a formal diagnosis, barriers that once felt insurmountable began to fall. What had seemed like an endless maze of obstacles slowly became a path forward. Accessing essential services, making necessary modifications and accommodations, setting goals, advocating, and developing strategies, which once felt overwhelming, became much more manageable. Understanding Landon's unique challenges enabled me to advocate for him more effectively and fostered stronger collaboration among his dedicated caregivers and educators, who were lifelines throughout his journey.

Through it all, beyond additional neurological and medical conditions we encountered over the years, I held on to hope—a constant guide through uncertainty. I never wavered in my belief that I was making the right choices:

seeking the necessary diagnoses, assembling a strong support system, and creating a structured plan tailored to Landon's needs. Over time, that support team became more than just professionals—they became family. Teachers, aides, bus drivers, coaches, therapists, and medical experts all played vital roles, their dedication shaping not just Landon's progress but my own growth as well.

Yet, the thought that lingers in my mind daily—the one that consumes me most—is that I won't always be here to guide him. The weight of that reality is immense. Life is unpredictable, and I know I must prepare Landon for a future where I might not be by his side. Like many parents, I worry—about the success he will achieve, the challenges he will face, the relationships he will build, the skills he will need to navigate adulthood, and the family he will create. Yet, within that worry lies my deepest resolve.

My purpose remains unchanged: to love, teach, empower, and encourage him, always. I want Landon to carry within him an unshakable sense of self-worth and resilience, knowing he is capable of reaching his dreams— no matter how distant they may seem. Our days are filled with learning, laughter, communication, and growth, each moment adding another brick to the foundation I am building for him.

Every time I see Landon succeed—whether he's solving a challenging puzzle, achieving a new high score in bowling, learning a new recipe, adding another piece of artwork to his portfolio, facing his fears by asking a friend to prom, or finding new ways to express himself—my heart swells with pride. These victories, big or small, serve as constant reminders of his strength, courage, and limitless potential.

Yet, amid all my efforts to prepare him for the future, I cherish the present. He is the one person I could never imagine my life without—the light that fills my days. His laughter brings warmth to our home, his smile eases my fears, and his curiosity about the world never ceases to inspire me. I find joy in our shared experiences, whether it's the quiet evenings spent watching our favorite shows, facing the challenges of visiting doctor after doctor, or spending long days traveling to tournaments. Each moment is a treasure and a glimpse into the future I hope for him.

As we continue this journey, I remind myself that my role is not just to prepare him for a life without me, but to help him build a life rich with love, empowerment, experience, and understanding. I want him to live fully and joyfully. I envision a future where he is surrounded by a network of support—friends, mentors, and advocates who will stand by him, just as I do now.

Ultimately, this is a journey of love—love for Landon, for his future, for our bond, for everyone who will enter and remain in his life, and for the unyielding spirit that blossoms within him. Even when I am no longer physically present, I hope my lessons, values, and unconditional love will continue to guide and support him. Hope is not just a feeling; it is an active force, shaping our lives with every choice we make. And as we move forward, I trust that my unwavering belief in Landon—and the love that fuels it—will forever light his path, even in the darkest of times.

CHAPTER *5*

~~~~~

Unveiling the Inner Warrior

A Journey of Challenge and Resilience

Adjusting to our new life felt like relearning how to ride a bike—wobbly at first but filled with small victories. Each day brought new achievements. I found myself changing our approach and strategies repeatedly: Some things worked, and some things didn't, and I knew that to find our path, I had to keep shifting as we moved forward. He was navigating life on his own terms, and I fully embraced that. My heart swelled with joy at every milestone achieved. I was getting my little boy back. Therapy was working, teachers were teaching how he learned, doctors were listening, and I savored every precious moment.

Gradually, life settled into a rhythm. It wasn't the path I had envisioned when I first became a mother, but it was ours. And he was mine. That realization sent warmth rushing through me—not a surge of adrenaline, but an overwhelming sense of love and gratitude. Landon's presence in my life made me certain of one thing: no challenge could break us. As long as we were together, no obstacle was too great, no puzzle too difficult. The pieces of our journey might not always fit perfectly, but with love at the center, we would continue building something beautiful.

Yet, as Landon grew, new struggles emerged. More diagnoses, more unanswered questions. Just when I thought we were nearing solid ground, another wave would push us further out to sea. It felt like we were being tested, as if someone expected us to fail. There were moments I wanted to give in—but my heart wouldn't let me. Deep down, I believed that some of his conditions overlapped with autism, but his young age made a definitive evaluation impossible at the time.

Doctors diagnosed Landon with dysgraphia, dyspraxia, anxiety, and attention deficit hyperactivity disorder (ADHD)-inattentive type—in addition to autism. Navigating these challenges has been overwhelming, but each new step brings its own lessons and strengths. Despite the difficulties, I know that my love for Landon and the unbreakable bond we share will help us overcome whatever obstacles lie ahead. Together, we will continue to adapt and thrive, no matter how complex the journey becomes.

Dysgraphia

Landon has always had a vivid imagination. From the moment he could hold a crayon, he filled page after page with colorful drawings that made his world come alive. But when it came to writing, that vibrant creativity faded into frustration.

To help him, I turned our writing sessions into a playful experience. I set up a cozy space in the living room, surrounding him with his favorite art supplies and stacks of bright paper. I encouraged him to trace letters while doodling freely, blending his love for art with the challenge of writing.

At first, I—and many others who worked with Landon believed his struggles came from weak fine motor  skills. His grip on pencils and pens was unsteady, making letters wobble across the page in an unintentional dance. But it wasn't just the mechanics of writing that frustrated him. Trying to put his thoughts onto paper felt like catching smoke with bare hands—a fleeting idea that vanished before he could hold onto it.

Writing assignments became a source of frustration for Landon, leaving him discouraged before every stroke with his pencil. I often found him sitting at his Toy Story desk, staring at a blank page as his thoughts swirled into a chaotic storm—so many ideas, yet the right words remained just out of reach. He wandered through his sentences, trapped in a maze of his own making, only to emerge exhausted, often giving up before he could truly begin.

Recognizing his struggle, I took a different approach. I'd ask questions, guessing what he might be thinking to help him get the words on paper. Sitting beside him, I gently guided his hand over the letters, helping him feel their shapes as we traced them together. Tracing paper became a favorite tool, allowing him to outline both letters and pictures. Writing practice turned into an adventure—squishing Playdough into letter shapes, tracing words with our fingers in a bin of rice, fingerpainting, and discovering new ways to make learning feel natural rather than forced.

As our lessons continued, I introduced fresh ideas, like using colorful markers to draw oversized letters on different sizes of paper. We made a game of it—I'd write a letter, and he'd race to find an object in the room that started with the same sound. Once he found the object, he'd come back to the table to trace the letter. The air filled with laughter, the weight of learning lifting as fun took over.

One day, as we shaped letters with Playdough, Landon pointed proudly to his creation. *"Wook, Mommy! 'L'!"* His eyes sparkled with excitement, and in that moment, joy surged through me. Besides creating the letter, he understood its relation to his own name. What once seemed like a simple distraction had become a tool for discovery. Slowly, a flicker of confidence emerged.

With each session, we added new elements—stencils, colored sand, slime, glue, even glitter. What had once been a source of frustration became a world of exploration. Landon started initiating writing challenges, eager to create more projects together.

By the time our lessons had stretched into months, he wasn't just writing letters—he was creating art with them, blending imagination with skill. He began writing one line sentences. The struggle faded into the background, replaced by a journey of creativity and self-expression.

As his writing developed, the letters on the page grew more recognizable. The once big, squiggly shapes took form, though he still faced challenges with spacing and punctuation, often mixing uppercase and lowercase letters. Yet, amidst those weaknesses, he excelled at spelling. It became his strength—a glimmer of achievement that lifted his spirits and nurtured a growing sense of self-worth.

He loved the thrill of learning new words and mastering their spellings. With each word I introduced, he visualized the letters dancing in his mind, his excitement building as he carefully spelled them aloud. Before I could even clap, he was already twirling in circles and flapping his hands with delight. When he heard me cheer and saw me throw my arms up, he rushed in for a hug, grinning, saying, and signing, *"More, please!"*

With every new word, his enthusiasm grew. He tackled "outside" and "train" with the same energy as "bat" and *"pig."* We turned our study sessions into playful competitions, where every correct spelling earned a joyful jump or a silly dance.

Spelling became more than just homework—it turned into an adventure, a celebration of creativity and discovery. He eagerly used new words in conversations and play, sharing them with anyone or anything willing to listen. Watching his confidence bloom was incredibly rewarding. Writing down the words he had mastered became a fun challenge rather than a chore. *"More, Mommy!"* he would exclaim, eager for the next one.

In 2023, Landon was diagnosed with dysgraphia—a term that, at first, felt unfamiliar until I unraveled its meaning. I had long recognized his struggles, and finally having a name for them brought understanding, compassion, and clarity. It opened doors to new resources and support.

Dysgraphia is a learning disorder that affects writing skills. Children with dysgraphia often struggle to hold writing tools properly and form letters due to motor difficulties. It also impacts key writing elements such as spelling, grammar, punctuation, sentence structure, and the ability to translate thoughts onto paper. What Landon can express effortlessly in conversation may become jumbled and difficult to write, leading to resistance, frustration and discouragement.

After his diagnosis, we adjusted his learning environment to better support his needs. We introduced adaptive tools and specialized activities aimed at strengthening his writing abilities. I collaborated with his teachers, aide, therapists, and the case manager to ensure he received essential accommodations, such as extra time for assignments and tests, preferential seating, and the option to use technology for note-taking. The team embraced these changes wholeheartedly, eager to help him succeed. They provided graphic organizers, pre-printed notes, step by step instructions, and allowed him to present his work in various formats—verbal responses, presentations, or videos—giving him the opportunity to demonstrate his understanding in ways that played to his strengths.

This shift in approach allowed Landon to focus on his ideas rather than getting overwhelmed by the mechanics of writing. He watched his thoughts take shape without the anxiety that had once accompanied written tasks. Gradually, his confidence grew, and he became more engaged in learning.

Throughout this journey, Landon's artistic flair remained a constant, radiating the same brilliance as his childhood scribbles. His drawings weren't just creative outlets; they were proof that each stroke of his pencil held boundless potential.

Through art, Landon's resilience became evident— not only in the struggles he faced with writing but in the victories he achieved along the way. Every challenge he overcame became a stepping stone, shaping a path filled with growth, support, and a vibrant spark of creativity. He learned to express himself through writing in his own way, embracing both his artistic talents and his distinct voice.

Despite the hurdles, Landon found joy in activities that fueled his creativity and imagination. He loved arranging blocks by color, weaving stories through his drawings, and swinging at the playground until the sun dipped below the horizon. Yet, when faced with tasks that felt too difficult, he often withdrew. Frustration would wash over him, convincing him that no amount of help could ease his struggle.

Some mornings, just the thought of the day ahead would bring him to tears. He knew the challenges waiting for him at school, and the weight of that anticipation made getting ready even harder. Simple tasks—putting on his coat, fastening his shoes—felt overwhelming. Sensing his unease, I sometimes pretended to struggle with my own shoes. Seeing me fumble would spark something in him—his instinct to help. He loved being useful. The moment he lent a hand, I would high-five him, pull him into a hug, and say, *"Thank you! You're so good at helping me. Maybe we can help each other with the things we find difficult."*

That day marked the beginning of a new approach. I turned practice into play, transforming frustrating tasks into lighthearted games. Whether it was zipping up his favorite jacket or weaving through an obstacle course on his bike, Landon slowly realized that asking for help wasn't a weakness—it was part of learning.

Helping others became his greatest joy. At home, at school, in the store, or at the park, he found fulfillment in simple tasks—zipping both our coats, organizing his toys, completing chores and homework, counting coins, and putting away groceries. These everyday moments became additions to our toolkit and proof of his progress, each one lighting up his face with pride. Praise wasn't just encouragement to him; it was a badge of honor, a sign that his efforts mattered.

He had learned that it was okay to seek support when things felt overwhelming. I reminded him often, *"Focus on what you can do, not just what you haven't mastered yet. And remember, everyone needs help sometimes. It takes courage to ask for it."* Through consistent communication and encouragement, he found a way to embrace his writing challenges until he mastered them. By showing him that I sometimes needed help, it encouraged him to ask for it too.

With those words in his heart, Landon no longer shied away from tasks that once seemed impossible. He understood that in facing them, he didn't have to do it alone. Step by step, he gained independence— navigating stairs on his own, riding his bike a little longer, getting dressed without assistance, buttoning his coat with ease, and asking for help on writing assignments. And in those moments, he realized that his journey wasn't just about overcoming obstacles—it was about discovering the joy of learning and growing at his own pace.

As the years passed, Landon continued to flourish. He discovered that his resilience was a strength that propelled him forward. With the love and support surrounding him daily, he gained the confidence to confront any challenges that came his way. Each day offered a new opportunity to learn, grow, and shine, leaving behind a trail of success and hope for those who admired him.

Anxiety

Although Landon struggled with social cues, he had always been a perceptive child, quick to notice subtle shifts in people's moods and the unspoken emotions behind their expressions. If I was sad, he knew it, and there's no way to deny it. However, his heightened awareness was a double-edged sword. While he eagerly participated in playground games and classroom discussions, a quiet storm of worry often loomed beneath his enthusiasm.

From a young age, his mind was a whirlwind of anxious "what if" questions—both improbable and painfully plausible. These thoughts weren't fleeting worries; they clung to him, pressing down on his shoulders in moments when others seemed carefree.

While his peers navigated childhood fears with ease, Landon found himself caught in an exhausting web of overthinking. He struggled to describe how his heart raced at the thought of school assignments, how his stomach knotted when he had to speak in front of a group, or the moments he had to see me leave, needing reassurance that I would return.

At first, I tried to soothe his fears with logic, not fully grasping how deeply his anxiety ran. I'd reassure him, telling him everything would be fine, that his fears were unlikely to come true. But it wasn't that simple. His emotions weren't just nerves; they were all-consuming.

Eventually, we received a diagnosis—generalized anxiety, separation anxiety, and somatic anxiety. With that came a bittersweet relief: understanding. Yet, as his mother, I felt powerless, caught in the storm of his emotions, desperately searching for a way to anchor him.

That diagnosis marked a turning point. I was determined to explore every possible solution before resorting to medication, mindful of the potential side effects. Instead, I turned to alternative methods, hoping to equip Landon with tools to navigate his anxiety in a sustainable way.

I created a haven of holistic practices tailored to his needs. We explored behavioral therapies, introduced mindfulness techniques, and made small but meaningful lifestyle changes. Every day, I encouraged him to practice deep breathing, a skill taught by many but mastered only with time and patience. Journaling became a vital part of his routine, offering him a safe outlet to untangle the emotions he struggled to express aloud. Every day, I began adding handwritten affirmations to his lunch bag to comfort him throughout the day.

As he grew older, adolescence brought new challenges. Making friends, which had once come easily, became increasingly difficult. Middle school tested him in ways I never anticipated. Bullying became a cruel reality, leaving scars on his self-esteem and sense of safety. The humiliation of being targeted made him doubt himself, especially since he had always led with kindness. It broke my heart to see him grapple with the painful truth that not everyone shared his values—that cruelty could exist where he had hoped for compassion.

We talked often during those difficult days. I reminded him that friendships are fluid—people enter our lives for different reasons, and losing connections doesn't define who we are. Each interaction, whether uplifting or painful, deepened his understanding of relationships, helping him appreciate those who genuinely cared and release those who didn't.

Even at his lowest points, Landon's true nature shined through. He was kind, approachable, and effortlessly inspiring. Those who knew him saw the warmth in his spirit, the way he lifted others even when burdened with his own struggles.

As challenges continued to weigh on him, I knew we needed to take further action. Without hesitation, Landon chose to pursue counseling—a decision I wholeheartedly supported. While I wished I could shield him from every hardship, I understood that the greatest gift I could offer was the freedom to explore his own solutions with professional guidance by his side.

After careful research, we found a therapist whose warmth immediately put him at ease. Therapy became his sanctuary—a space where he could unburden his heart and navigate his emotions without fear of judgment. Encouraged to express himself fully, he developed coping strategies that strengthened his resilience.

A key turning point in his journey was learning to set personal goals. Small victories became stepping stones, helping him adapt to a world that never stopped shifting. He stopped chasing perfection and, instead, embraced his true self, recognizing mistakes as opportunities to grow.

At first, he was hesitant about attending sessions alone, but over time, he grew more comfortable. My presence in his sessions, when invited, reassured him that he wasn't alone. He came to understand that while he couldn't control the actions of others, he could always nurture his own thoughts and responses—an empowering realization that would guide him forward.

Watching him advocate for himself has been one of my proudest moments. Years of open conversations and support had built a foundation upon which he now stood with confidence. Seeing him take ownership of his decisions filled my heart with pride.

Through both joyful and challenging moments, I continue to remind Landon that his journey is uniquely his own, and I am honored to walk beside him. Together, we've uncovered a simple yet powerful truth—life's uncertainties may come and go, but he carries the strength to face whatever lies ahead with courage and dignity. Each day is an adventure, and Landon is learning to embrace it head-on, discovering what it truly means to live.

Attention Deficit Hyperactivity Disorder – Inattentive

From a young age, Landon saw the world through a unique lens—one that was both vibrant and overwhelming. As he grew, his struggles became more pronounced, leading to an early diagnosis of Pervasive Developmental Disorder – Not Otherwise Specified, a condition commonly linked to

Asperger's syndrome. But as he entered adolescence, it became clear that a reevaluation was necessary.

Unfortunately, his previous neurologist moved, so I had to find another doctor for Landon. It was a bright Monday morning when we walked into the doctor's office. I was carrying a thick folder with reports from his teachers and therapists and my records. This long-awaited appointment would hopefully bring more clarity to Landon's recent experiences. With advances in medical research, his initial diagnosis no longer fit, and the medical community had since refined its classifications. It was time to update Landon's diagnosis to Autism Spectrum Disorder (ASD).

As we sat in the waiting room, Landon fidgeted with the hem of his shirt, his eyes flicking nervously between the framed pictures on the walls. Sensing his unease, I leaned in with a reassuring smile.

"You're going to do great, baby. The doctor is just going to give you a checkup."

His voice was small, edged with worry. *"No needles, Mommy?"*

I saw the fear in his deep brown eyes. Landon had always been terrified of needles—a fear rooted in past experiences that had been far from gentle. The countless shots and blood draws had left a lasting mark, each one replaying in his mind like an echo of distress.

I gently took his hand, giving it a reassuring squeeze. *"I promise, honey, there won't be any needles today. Just a little talking and some light checking to make sure you're healthy."*

His shoulders slowly relaxed, the tension easing as he absorbed my words.

After a thorough assessment, the doctor confirmed what I had long suspected—Landon not only met the criteria for Autism Spectrum Disorder (ASD) but also had Attention Deficit Hyperactivity Disorder (ADHD), inattentive type. Unlike hyperactive ADHD, the inattentive form is marked by difficulties with focus, organization, and attention. Individuals with this condition often struggle to stay engaged in tasks, easily sidetracked by external distractions or their own wandering thoughts.

As the doctor listed the associated traits—his tendency to fidget, moments of zoning out, failing to stay on topic, and emotional struggles—I nodded, a mixture of relief and concern settling over me. Over the years, I had noticed how sensory overload often triggered these behaviors, yet many mistook them for impulsiveness or defiance.

I also knew that ADHD and ASD frequently overlapped, so the additional diagnosis didn't come as a shock. I had read countless studies linking the two, and the pieces fit. Landon's struggles with focus, his mind jumping from one thought to another like a butterfly flitting from flower to flower—it all made sense now.

For some, another label might feel overwhelming, but for me, it was another piece of the puzzle. It explained why even the faintest sounds could pull him away from a task, why his attention drifted in the middle of conversations, why structure and routine were so essential for him. This newfound understanding wasn't just about naming his challenges—it was about finding better ways to support him.

But then, the doctor mentioned medication.

Casually, almost as if it were a foregone conclusion, he handed me a prescription. I stiffened.

I knew medication could be life-changing for some children, but this felt rushed, as if it were the only solution. Landon didn't need a quick fix—he needed tools, strategies, and support to navigate his emotions and manage his sensory experiences.

"Let's hold off on medication for now," I said, keeping my tone even though irritation simmered beneath the surface. I didn't want to dismiss the doctor's expertise

outright, but the ease with which the prescription was offered unsettled me. *"I think we should explore some strategies first."*

The doctor studied me for a moment before nodding. *"That's perfectly reasonable,"* he said, tapping his pen against his notepad. *"Many parents start with medication before considering behavioral strategies."*

I met his gaze, a quiet determination rising in me. *"I'm not most parents,"* I said after a pause. *"And I have my reasons for approaching things differently."* The words hung between us, firm but respectful.

I wasn't rejecting medical advice. I wasn't dismissing the possibility that medication could one day help. But I knew my child. And I knew, beyond any doubt, that he needed more than a prescription—he needed understanding, patience, and a world that embraced him for who he was.

The words lingered in the air, and I watched as the doctor processed my response. For years, I had advocated for Landon and his unique needs, often feeling like an outlier. The idea of resorting to medication before fully exploring behavioral strategies gnawed at me.

"I've seen how Landon responds best to approaches that prioritize understanding his experiences," I said, my

voice steadier now. *"There's so much we can learn from his behaviors to help him thrive."*

The doctor nodded slowly, a flicker of respect in his eyes. *"It's clear you've put a lot of thought into this, and your dedication to Landon's well-being is commendable."* His words softened the tension, and I felt a glimmer of relief.

"I just want to be sure we're choosing what's best for him, not what's easiest," I added, my heart pounding. The weight of my conviction carried every word, and I knew I had to stand firm for Landon.

At school, Landon had a well-structured Individualized Education Plan (IEP) in place. His teachers and therapists were incredible—implementing strategies like frequent breaks, one-on-one support, sensory aids to help him adapt to the classroom, and consistent communication. They understood his needs, fostering an inclusive and supportive environment where he could grow.

Yet, despite their efforts, he thrived most in quieter settings— like the comfort of our home, where distractions were minimal, and he could focus on what truly engaged him. There was something grounding about the stillness of our house, the soft glow of the afternoon sun casting warm light across the floor, illuminating the little fragments of his world—his trains, WWE figures, Legos, art supplies, picture books, and the puzzle books he had grown so fond of.

I watched in awe as he flourished. With each passing day, he grew more confident, embracing his unique perspective on life. The adjustments at home and school provided a safe space, allowing him to explore his interests and talents. Together, we navigated this journey with understanding and faith in his potential, grateful for the community that supported him, enabling him to thrive.

CHAPTER *6*

Navigating the Medical System

Since the moment Landon was born, my life shifted into a series of doctor, therapy and hospital visits. From his time in the NICU to battling consistent fevers, various viruses, ear infections, pneumonia, and even a vaccination injury, it felt like I was living in a world dominated by medical appointments and uncertainty. The hospital staff guided me through each challenge with care and expertise, equipping me with knowledge I didn't know I needed.

This was not the life I had envisioned for my son. I had dreamed of joyful milestones, laughter-filled days, and a carefree childhood. While I did experience many of those moments, savoring each one, I found myself navigating an unexpected reality. A mix of fear, grace, and determination accompanied each visit to the hospital or a new specialist. These trips became lessons and opportunities to learn not only about Landon's health but also about resilience.

I quickly realized that I had no choice but to adapt. I immersed myself in understanding medical terminology and processes, asking questions, and seeking clarity whenever possible. Most nurses and doctors treated Landon with care, and I formed a bond with them—people who understood our struggles and offered unwavering support. Yet, not all interactions with medical personnel were comforting, and during those moments of disconnect, I knew it was essential to find those who truly prioritized compassionate care.

There were days filled with anxiety when the weight of uncertainty felt nearly unbearable. Yet, amidst the fear, I discovered the value of learning, the grace of patience, and the power of hope. Every hug, kiss, and smile from Landon, every small attempt and victory, became a reminder that we were not defined by his struggles but by our ability to face them together.

As we confronted each challenge, I learned to celebrate the victories: a successful vaccination, a fever that subsided, a successful surgery, or a doctor's positive report. These moments fueled my resolve to advocate for Landon, to be his voice when he couldn't speak for himself.

Through it all, I found a strength within me that I never knew existed. The journey was not what I had planned, but it was rich with love, authenticity, learning and growth.

And although I often wished for a different path, I embraced our reality with open arms, grateful for every moment that brought us closer together as a family.

As we continued navigating this unpredictable journey, doctors diagnosed Landon with food and environmental allergies, gastroesophageal reflux disease (GERD), achalasia, prediabetes, Wolff-Parkinson-White Syndrome (WPW Syndrome), and currently under evaluation for orthostatic hypotension before a diagnosis can be made. Each diagnosis felt like a blow, sending waves of fear and uncertainty through me.

I often found myself gasping for air, struggling to process one relentless challenge after another. How did this happen? Why did no one discover this sooner? I desperately wished I could rewind time to those days in the doctor's office, hoping to negotiate my way out of this grim fate.

What are our next steps moving forward? I often find myself at a crossroads, reflecting on the possibilities and striving to identify the most effective course of action. Is it curable or lifelong? I often paced, my breath quickening as I pondered whether his condition was something he could overcome or if we would be forced to navigate this shadowy landscape for the rest of his life. The uncertainty gnawed at me—a persistent companion that made it difficult to breathe.

With each new diagnosis, the weight of responsibility pressed down on me, and the need to learn became urgent. I dove into research, reading everything I could find and asking all the questions I could think of. My days blurred together, filled with appointments, tests, and consultations, but I clung to every shred of hope and every small victory.

Allergies and Dietary Changes

Landon brought so much love, laughter, and energy into our home, but he was silently battling discomfort. It all began with his first sip of whole milk just after turning one year old. Persistent eczema and nights filled with distress disrupted his otherwise joyful days. As a concerned mother, I sought answers through a food allergy test, feeling both hopeful and anxious. When the results revealed allergies to milk, egg whites, peanuts, soybeans, and corn, it felt like a missing piece of a puzzle had fallen into place. We removed these foods from his diet, hoping for a future where he could find comfort and joy again.

As the weeks passed, we saw some improvement in Landon, but it wasn't the miracle we had hoped for. His discomfort lingered, dimming his spirit and making laughter a rare occurrence. Heartbroken, I decided it was time to consult a gastroenterologist for a deeper investigation into his consistent stomach aches.

On the day of the appointment, I held Landon's hand tightly, a mix of hope and apprehension filling the air. The doctor was warm and suggested a colonoscopy, endoscopy, and blood tests. While I was nervous about Landon needing anesthesia and being pricked again, I also felt a sense of relief—finally, we were taking steps to uncover the source of his discomfort and restore his vibrant spirit.

Landon underwent both a colonoscopy and an endoscopy at three years old. He felt so scared lying on the operating table. The bright lights, beeping equipment, and unfamiliar faces only heightened his anxiety. I held his hand until he fell asleep, and I couldn't help but tear up as I watched him drift off. My heart broke at the thought of him being too young to go through all of this.

After the procedure, the doctor informed us that Landon did well, and she discovered he had irritable bowel syndrome (IBS), gastroesophageal reflux disease (GERD), and some inflammation in his digestive tract.

I asked about the cause of the inflammation, and the doctor explained that she had taken a biopsy to send to the lab. Days later, the results indicated that lactose intolerance might be contributing to his issues. The potential answer was close but not certain.

The thought of lactose intolerance was daunting for Landon, especially since he loved cheese. Acknowledging the need for change, we started an elimination diet under medical guidance, removing dairy products to see if it alleviated his symptoms. He was prescribed Prilosec for acid reflux, Lactaid to aid in dairy digestion, and Miralax for constipation.

The first few weeks were challenging but also filled with discoveries of dairy-free alternatives, which provided some relief from his symptoms. However, as time went on, the discomfort returned, prompting me to seek advice from another allergist.

In 2011, Landon was anxious about his allergy test, fearing needles. To help ease his nerves, I took him outside to distract him. He found comfort in watching geese walk across the parking lot. To further take his mind off the upcoming appointment, I pulled out some animal crackers from my bag so he could feed the geese, and his face lit up with excitement. I wanted to distract him as much as possible, even though I knew this calm wouldn't last long. When it was finally time for the test, he tensed up, began kicking and screaming, and even managed to bite my collarbone.

As we walked into the room, he held on to me tightly. The nurse checked his vitals while he sat on my lap, refusing to let go. The doctor entered, greeted us, and after listening to my concerns, she examined Landon. He was tense the entire time, flinching at the sight of anything the doctor took out. Before proceeding, she explained that the allergy test would not involve needles; instead, only liquid drops would be placed on his skin. As she demonstrated what would happen by using drops of water on my hand, his body relaxed, and his smile lit up the room. A few moments later, the test was performed.

A while later, the doctor and nurse returned with results that made my heart sink. Words like "goat's milk," "egg whites," "cow's milk," and "maize" felt like heavy stones in my stomach. *"What happened to the other allergies?" "Where did the new ones come from in such a short time."* I asked, concerned.

The doctor explained that the body can sometimes adapt to certain foods, while at other times it may reject them. I was alarmed by how quickly allergies can change, leaving me with a new list of foods to avoid after years of managing soy and peanut allergies. This made the process more challenging, as I was uncertain whether I needed to continue avoiding the foods that he had previously been allergic to.

As we left, Landon innocently asked, *"Can I have my cheese now?"* I wanted to shield him from sadness, but I had to be completely honest with him and stay firm on the rules. *"Not yet, baby, but you can still eat your new cheese,"* I said sadly. Strict vigilance became our routine until I could figure out what was really going on.

At home, the kitchen turned into a lab. I read labels meticulously, tried new recipes, and spent hours experimenting to create safe versions of his favorite dishes. I made sure to have pre-made food on hand. Despite my efforts, feeding him became increasingly difficult. He rejected most foods due to their appearance, texture, temperature, and now taste.

In 2012, while snacking on a mix of nuts and berries, Landon's lips began to swell. At first, I thought he was simply satisfied but soon panic set in as I realized he was struggling to breathe. I rushed him to the emergency room, where the doctors quickly stabilized him. A follow-up allergy test confirmed my worst fears: he was allergic to tree nuts, specifically almonds. *"What is happening? He just had an allergy test, and his peanut allergy was no longer present.*

In fact, nuts didn't even show up," I asked the doctor, feeling overwhelmed by the uncertainty.

After learning that such issues can occur, his pediatrician decided to conduct another allergy test, which confirmed an allergy to tree nuts. To explore his ongoing stomach problems, the pediatrician also ordered a celiac panel. While the test returned negative, it showed a precursor I had never heard of. What did this mean?

Motivated by concern and curiosity, I researched celiac disease and gluten intolerance and learned about its complexities. I realized the importance of adjusting our diet—becoming skilled at reading labels and cooking gluten- and casein-free meals. This transformation in our kitchen led to significant improvements in Landon's health—his stomach aches decreased, his bloated belly flattened, he moved more freely, and his behavior became more engaging and expressive. He was starting to feel better.

For nearly three years, I maintained his strict diet while avoiding other allergens. Then, we received the joyful news that Landon was allergy-free! However, reintroducing certain foods caused his stomach issues to return, leading to confusion and frustration. After several dietary attempts, we reintroduced MiraLax while limiting dairy and gluten, which provided some relief. For years it was a constant battle trying to solve a problem that offered minimal to no solution.

In early 2023, a visit to the allergist revealed new environmental sensitivities and food allergies to rice, barley, and dairy, alongside gluten sensitivity and, yet again, a precursor for celiac disease. This was a heavy blow, but we quickly removed the problematic foods from his diet. Landon took charge of his health, learning to read labels, and discovered a love for primarily vegan and plant-based foods.

Finding specialty items became easier after a new grocery store opened nearby, and his environmental allergies improved thanks to allergy shots. During his follow-up appointment, the doctor suggested potentially reintroducing the foods he had previously been allergic to if the tests came back negative. However, they did not show up as negative. Landon confidently and politely stated that even if the tests had come back negative, he would continue to avoid those foods, acknowledging the improvements in his health.

This journey wasn't just another dietary shift; it became a holistic lifestyle transformation for Landon. Through these challenges, resilience had emerged, and with every change made, Landon not only found relief from his past struggles but also embraced a new way of living—one that prioritized his safety and well-being while celebrating the joy of discovering new, nourishing foods he loved.

Achalasia

A challenging time began for Landon in 2020 during the COVID-19 pandemic. It started subtly with a slight hesitation at meals, but gradually, it grew into a more pressing concern. At first, I tried not to worry. Landon insisted he was fine, his trademark calmness masking the underlying difficulties. Yet, my instincts urged me to pay closer attention, unaware of the challenges that lay ahead.

As I watched him quietly struggle, a knot of worry tightened in my stomach. His past sensitivity to certain textures and temperatures resurfaced in my mind along with the possibility of new allergens. I recalled his tendency to pocket food in his cheeks like a squirrel storing acorns—an odd habit that, though quirky, now felt like a troubling omen.

As time passed, cutting his food into bite-sized pieces became our method to reduce his choking risk and allow the food to pass with ease. Landon had always savored his meals, taking each bite with careful deliberation. To him, food was not just nourishment; it was an experience to be enjoyed, rich in both flavor and nutrition.

Despite our cautious efforts, Landon's struggles intensified. Gagging and vomiting became more frequent, and I found myself gripped with panic each time he choked or tried to expel the contents of his mouth. Each episode served as a sharp reminder of how fragile our approach to eating had become. Liquids, too, presented challenges.

The weight of these developments pressed heavily on my heart. It was clear that Landon's relationship with food had shifted from enjoyment to anxiety. An acute fear took root, undermining his ability to maintain a healthy weight and leaving him looking more fragile each day.

Recognizing the gravity of the situation, I took a deep breath and called his doctor. My urgent tone prompted swift action, and Landon was referred to a gastroenterologist whose expertise would help guide us through this confusing terrain. After a thorough examination, the doctor expressed concern that Landon might have achalasia, a rare disorder that affects the nerves of the esophagus, making swallowing progressively more difficult.

I took a moment to process the word. Achalasia. It felt foreign on my tongue, a distant concept that suddenly became terrifyingly close. *"What the hell is Achalasia?"* I found myself asking, desperation creeping into my voice. *"How did this escalate so quickly without being found? Is it genetic, linked to allergies, or something else?"*

The doctor explained that achalasia is often an insidious condition, sometimes misdiagnosed until it reaches a more severe stage. He detailed the symptoms, painting a picture of how Landon's body had been silently struggling, warning signs masked by life's daily bustle. The thought that my son had been enduring this alone was unbearable.

Just before Christmas 2021, after a year of difficulties and consultations, Landon underwent an esophagram, which is a barium swallow test used for diagnostic imaging to evaluate the esophagus during swallowing. The procedure went smoothly once Landon understood the expectations. We received the results immediately, confirming the doctor's suspicions, although more procedures were needed to diagnose him accurately. Hoping for answers, an endoscopy was scheduled urgently.

The day of the procedure arrived, and as we waited in the sterile, brightly lit room, anxiety hung thick in the air. The endoscopy was fairly quick and revealed significant inflammation and narrowing of Landon's esophagus—a troubling finding that cast a shadow over our hopes.

Landon's doctor still couldn't be sure but suspected the rare condition, achalasia, might be the cause. To investigate further, he collaborated with another gastroenterologist who had expertise with the disease. They recommended an additional test, an esophageal manometry, which could confirm their suspicions. I vividly remember the surge of hope and fear that overwhelmed me in that moment. This could be the clarity we had been desperately seeking, yet part of me wished it weren't true.

However, the thought of the test itself was daunting. It required a thin tube to be inserted through Landon's nose, down the back of his throat, and into his esophagus—all while he would remain fully awake. The day of the test became one of the hardest moments I've ever witnessed. I tried my best to comfort him, holding his hand and offering words of reassurance, but I could see the distress building on his face. The medical team attempted the procedure four times, each attempt leaving him more exhausted and defeated.

Just when it seemed like we couldn't bear it anymore, they gathered their determination for one final try. Tears blurred my vision as the tube descended, each inch feeling like a fresh wave of grief for the intrusion into his innocent body. *"You're so brave. You're almost done. I got you. Just keep breathing through it,"* I whispered. Finally, they succeeded. Relief washed over us as the test was completed, but my heart ached for Landon, who had endured so much.

"Mom," he whispered, his voice trembling, *"Are they all... finished? Is it over? I can't do this anymore."* His words came out softly, his eyes glistening with unshed tears. My voice shook as I choked out a hesitant *"yes,"* tears welling up in my eyes. *"And you did amazing; I'm so proud of you."* Hanging his head, he quietly apologized to everyone for the delay, the weight of his words hanging heavy in the air. The sight of his quiet struggle broke my heart—he couldn't see his own bravery, but we made sure to offer him words of encouragement.

Once the results came in, we learned that Landon was suffering from achalasia, a rare condition in which the esophagus loses the ability to move food into the stomach. Specifically, it affects the lower esophageal sphincter, a muscle that normally relaxes to allow food to pass. In Landon's case, this muscle failed to relax properly, significantly reducing the esophagus' muscle activity. Achalasia results from the deterioration and paralysis of the nerves within the esophagus, causing immense difficulty in eating and drinking.

While the diagnosis was overwhelming, there was also a sense of relief in finally understanding what he was facing. Everything in me wished he didn't have to, but here we were. I remember the doctor discussing potential treatments and reassuring us that help was available. It was too much to process—the information, emotions, and tests to confirm what was going on with my son.

Doctors emphasized the urgency of Landon's condition, recommending surgery to restore his ability to eat and drink. His journey began with the extraction of his wisdom teeth, which required a hospital stay and anesthesia. Although the recovery was uncomfortable, the pain was manageable, though his limited diet felt restrictive.

Just two weeks after the wisdom teeth surgery, Landon faced another dietary challenge—a strict 48-hour clear liquid diet. He saw this as an opportunity to experiment, finding comfort in clear broth and refreshing juices while avoiding Jello and Italian ice due to their textures and temperature.

The night before his surgery, apprehension began to settle in. Anxiety gripped him. Fear flooded me. Landon was scheduled for a Peroral Endoscopic Myotomy (POEM), a procedure that could change everything.

"What if they can't fix me?" he whispered to me. As I tried to hold back tears, I confidently said, *"They will. Remember, we have to think positive. The doctors are going to help you, baby."* The thought crept in, full of doubt. What

if the doctors' steady hands faltered, or if the procedure wouldn't work as intended?

He closed his eyes tightly, clutching the fabric of his shirt, attempting to dispel the growing fear. He had focused for so long on the hope of being able to eat regular meals again and drink without the choking anxiety. It felt like a dream that was just out of reach.

The surgery lasted nearly 1.5 hours, but to me, it felt like an eternity. As the anesthesia wore off, he slowly regained consciousness. The bright overhead lights were almost blinding, and the sterile scent of the hospital filled his senses. Disorientation clouded his mind as he tried to process where he was.

Then came the realization of the pain—a sharp, throbbing discomfort radiating from his chest and stomach. The nurses promptly responded and administered Tylenol to help ease his pain. Before he drifted back to sleep, he turned his head and saw his dad and me. The faintest of smiles touched his lips, and my heart ached with a familiar warmth, recognizing that everything he needed was right there, next to him.

Most of the day blurred into a haze of sleep and brief awakenings. Each time he roused from his drug-induced slumber, it was like walking through a fog; the pain would pull him back into the darkness. He would open his eyes to find me lying next to him, gently rubbing his hair, while his dad held his hand and smiled. Even in his discomfort, I could see that the moment brought him some comfort.

The nurses regularly checked Landon's vitals; their caring demeanor evident as he groaned in discomfort during the assessments. After administering Tylenol, he drifted back into a deep sleep. The following morning, the results of an esophagram brought smiles—the procedure was successful! Landon's heart soared with joy as he embraced the path to recovery.

"I'm all better now," his voice filled with excitement. *"Can I have something to drink please?"* he politely asked the doctor.

Cleared for clear liquids, he savored that first sip, appreciating the nourishment he had once taken for granted. As discharge approached, we felt hopeful about maintaining his health with annual check-ups and endoscopies. The nurses explained his post-operative care and diet, beginning with a clear liquid regimen of broths and gelatin, if desired, followed by creamy soups and smoothies. With renewed spirit, Landon looked forward to enjoying every meal and sip, eager to reclaim his quality of life.

However, the road to recovery wasn't without setbacks. Just a few days after returning home, Landon's father visited to check in on him and spend some time together. When it was time for his father to leave, Landon stood up to give him a hug goodbye. But when they separated, Landon suddenly collapsed. It all happened so quickly. I thought I reacted fast enough to catch him, but all I remember is screaming, "Call 911." The world seemed to blur into muted gray, and the sound faded into an aching silence.

The sickening thud of my son hitting the floor, face first echoed through my mind, mirroring the shattering of my heart. I gasped for breath in a world that seemed to lose its color. It felt like the moment in Rocky, seeing Apollo crumple to the floor, the crowd gasping, and a heavy silence replacing the roar. I burst into tears, screaming, *"Landon, baby, Landon!"*

He woke up in my arms, my hands cradling his head gently. *"Mommy, mommy, what happened?"* he asked, his voice full of confusion. Again, he whispered, *"Mommy,*

mommy, what happened? Mommy, Daddy, I'm okay, right?"
We reassured him, "Yes, baby, but the ambulance is on their
way. Just relax until they get here." He slightly shook his
head with concern in his eyes, "Mommy, why are you
crying? I'm okay." Despite everything, he seemed more
concerned about how we were feeling than about what had
just happened to him.

The paramedics arrived, and we told them Landon
had just had two surgeries in two weeks, and we believed
Landon had fainted due to malnourishment. My heart
stopped as I held his hand tightly in the ambulance. I
couldn't process what just happened. At the hospital, the
staff quickly assessed him and contacted his surgeon.
Fortunately, the doctors confirmed he had no serious injuries
and could recover at home, though the scare lingered in my
mind.

Back home, I watched Landon like a hawk, still
haunted by the image of him hitting the floor. Watching my
son collapse, his body suddenly limp, was a moment that
seared itself into my mind. The shock of it was
overwhelming, and for weeks afterward, I found myself
haunted by vivid flashbacks that played on an endless loop.

Each night, I was tormented by nightmares that left
me gasping for breath, feeling as if I were reliving that

heartbreaking scene. I couldn't shake off the image; it clung to me like a shadow. Tears would stream down my face at the most unexpected moments, and an anxious knot formed in my chest, tightening with every thought of that day.

A few days later, as he adjusted to a new diet of soft, pureed foods, I felt immense relief. His smile was infectious; it felt like witnessing a sunrise after a long night. His energy levels improved, but he took it easy until he could return to a normal diet again.

Over time, it became clear how much the surgery had changed him. He looked healthier and more vibrant, and laughter came more easily. This transformation filled me with joy, symbolizing a reclaiming of the quality of life he had almost lost. Each meal turned into a celebration, serving as a reminder to never take anything for granted.

Landon, who had long battled achalasia, was finally enjoying what we thought was a victory over his condition. However, that joy quickly faded as his symptoms returned, marking the beginning of another journey.

One evening in December 2023, we went out to dinner at a restaurant. We had become quite knowledgeable about what he could and could not eat to ensure he could enjoy the dining experience. However, after just a few bites, I noticed him looking at his food with distress.

He quietly said that everything was okay, but his look felt all too familiar, so I asked, *"Is the food getting stuck again?."* He nodded, explaining that it felt all too reminiscent of the struggles before his first surgery. Right after he explained, my heart sank as he ran to the bathroom to vomit violently, panic washing over him as he struggled to breathe during the choking episodes.

There was no exit for the food, and I could see the fear etched on his face. I knew I had to act fast, so I helped him expel the food. I called his doctor immediately to arrange for a comprehensive evaluation, fully aware of how profoundly this condition had impacted his life.

A few days after another esophagram, we learned that Landon's achalasia had resurfaced, making surgery unavoidable. In June 2024, during the surgery, his doctor discovered a Mallory-Weiss tear, which caused internal bleeding. Thankfully, it was addressed in time to prevent further complications.

As we headed toward the hospital's exit after his discharge, Landon, escorted in a wheelchair, broke into a smile, lighting up the shadows of uncertainty we had lived through for so long. He expressed heartfelt gratitude to his father and me, his doctor and all the nurses for caring for him, sharing a hopeful wish to avoid any more surgeries in the future.

I placed my hand on my heart and gently touched his face. *"I've got you; I always have and always will. I love you so much."* He looked at me knowingly and took my hand as we helped him into the car. We both held onto that moment as hope surged through my veins, firmly believing that this second surgery would help him manage his achalasia more effectively and guide us toward a healthier, brighter future together.

Over the next few weeks, Landon amazed us with his recovery. Despite following a strict diet of clear liquids and soft foods for more than a month, he embraced these changes with determination and resilience. He understood that short-term sacrifices were necessary for a brighter future.

Four months later, relief washed over us as we sat anxiously in the waiting room of the hospital for Landon's follow-up procedure. The endoscopy results revealed remarkable progress. Everything was heading in the right direction, just as the doctor had hoped and we prayed for. I couldn't help but feel overwhelmed with gratitude for the entire medical team.

Acknowledging that this disease is lifelong is daunting; not knowing where it will lead is frightening.

However, we remain hopeful that with treatment and our incredible medical team, we will find a way forward, one bite at a time.

Prediabetes

A few months after Landon's second surgery to treat his achalasia, life began to feel more normal. He was excited about the upcoming high school bowling season and was eager to get his yearly physical for clearance. The exam went well, and he was relieved to have maintained a healthy weight. The final step was a blood draw, which still made him anxious, but he had improved with needles since his earlier experiences.

When the nurse finished, he let out a relieved sigh. *"That wasn't so bad,"* he said with a smile, brushing off the stress of the visit. However, a few days later, his world was shaken by the blood work results, revealing that Landon's glucose level was a little high. The doctor ordered an A1C test to get a clearer picture, and the results revealed prediabetes. Considering Landon's dedication to healthy eating and thin physique, this news was unexpected and overwhelming.

Landon and I discussed the recent changes in his diet and agreed that the soft, convenient meals he had been eating might be contributing to his elevated blood sugar levels. As we looked over the selection of packaged, processed foods that had become staples in his meals, it became clear that their high sugar and carbohydrate content was problematic.

I suggested that we schedule a visit with his doctor to discuss potential dietary adjustments until he was cleared to eat whole foods again. I hoped this would be a crucial step in determining whether these dietary changes were a significant factor in his health concerns.

We explored a range of strategies to incorporate his favorite foods into his diet. Maintaining flavor while being mindful of texture was essential, as I didn't want to overwhelm him with drastic changes. We prepared grilled chicken and vibrant stir-fried vegetables, blending some components to make it more palatable, but the taste and smell were too much for his body to tolerate. Together, we planned to regain control over his eating habits, knowing this journey required both physical and emotional adjustments.

Fortunately, a few weeks later, Landon received clearance from his gastroenterologist to return to a healthier diet. He eagerly made a shopping list of his favorites— eggs, greens, fresh fruit, grilled chicken, protein bars and shakes, paleo waffles, water, salmon, cod, and more.

His healthcare provider recommended a low-glycemic diet, avoiding refined carbs and added sugar. With guidance from a nutritionist, we redesigned his meal plans to include more low-glycemic options, hoping to close this chapter and focus on his health.

As Landon prepared for his six-month follow-up blood test, he diligently adhered to his diet while incorporating an exercise regimen a few days a week. His dedication filled us with hope, even as we tried to push aside our fears about the results.

A text pinged my phone two days after his six-month blood work: the lab results were ready. When I signed into the portal to view the results, I read the disappointing news: Landon's A1C still showed prediabetes. After all the effort he had put in, it felt like we had hit a dead end, a brick wall. Landon was devastated. *"Why didn't it work?"* he asked quietly, almost to himself. The question hung in the air, heavy with the weight of his worries.

I knew how committed he had been to change his lifestyle—counting every carbohydrate, avoiding all food with added sugar, walking every day after school, and exchanging late-night snacks for water. *"Maybe I should've tried harder,"* he muttered, staring down at his hands. I comforted him, reminding him of the challenges he had already faced and encouraged him to stay positive. *"We will find a way forward, even if it takes time. We have to be patient."*

As I spoke, I noticed a hint of determination returning to his eyes. *"This is a learning process. Just because the results weren't what we hoped for doesn't mean we can't adjust and keep trying. Every step you take brings you closer to where you want to be."*

"Okay, Let's look into other options and figure out a better plan. I can do this." Landon finally said, his voice steadier.

Although this journey isn't over, we are learning to embrace it. Each setback serves as a lesson, and though we can't close this chapter just yet, we will write new pages filled with hope and resilience. We remain optimistic that with continued effort, Landon's prediabetes will remain steady or improve in the future.

Wolff-Parkinson-White Syndrome (WPW)

One day in November 2023, Landon came home from school with a furrowed brow, visibly distressed. When I asked what was wrong, he shared a troubling experience from gym class. That day, his class had done an intense Tabata Tuesday workout—high-intensity bursts of activity followed by brief rest intervals. Midway through, Landon felt dizzy and faint. He knew he had to sit down.

His heart raced, and he struggled to catch his breath as a pounding headache set in. Fatigue lingered long after class ended, prompting growing concern about his health. As I listened, a wave of worry swept over me. The symptoms sounded troubling, especially given our family's medical history.

"Did you tell anyone how you were feeling?" I asked. He shook his head "no," and I urged him to understand the importance of voicing his discomfort, especially in a school setting where help could be just a shout away. Speaking up could ensure that someone would step in and assess his condition, offering the support and care he needed.

Given the alarming nature of his symptoms, I quickly arranged for an evaluation with a pediatric cardiologist.

While I understood that overexertion could cause such reactions, these symptoms were unusual for a healthy teenager, and I wanted to prioritize caution. We sought to understand the situation better, ensuring both reassurance and proper care.

In December 2023, we walked into the softly lit cardiologist's office, apprehensive about what we might learn. The walls, adorned with heart health posters and framed certifications, offered little comfort as we awaited the doctor's arrival. When she entered, her demeanor was calm and composed, yet the weight of her presence seemed to amplify our anxiety.

After a thorough examination and a few thoughtful pauses, the doctor calmly delivered the diagnosis: Wolff-Parkinson-White syndrome (WPW)—an extra electrical pathway in the heart that could lead to episodes of rapid heartbeat. The words felt heavy, like a dense fog settling in.

At first, the abnormal EKG results confused us, but the echocardiogram offered a glimmer of hope. The images on the screen showed a healthy heart, which was reassuring. However, as the doctor explained WPW's implications—episodes of rapid heartbeats and potential supraventricular tachycardia (a condition where the heart beats faster than normal due to electrical disturbances)—the emotional weight grew heavier, leaving me unsettled.

Soon after, a nurse fitted him with a Zio Rhythm heart monitor, a small device that tracked his heart's rhythm continuously for a week. Every unusual sensation prompted him to reach for the button, each incident adding to his anxiety.

The cardiologist encouraged exercise to measure Landon's heart under strain, but after a few minutes of activity, he often showed concerning symptoms—wheezing, chest pain, and a glossiness in his eyes. Prioritizing his safety, I prompted him to stop or take breaks during workouts.

I made sure all school personnel knew his condition, creating a safety net for him during school hours. On the final day of monitoring, we sent the device back, and the doctor later reassured us that Landon's episodes were manageable without the need for medication or surgery.

Despite this reassurance, worry lingered as he experienced more episodes. Feeling uncertain, I sought a second opinion from another pediatric cardiologist, who recommended consulting with an electrophysiologist—a specialist in the electrical activities of the heart—to discuss the possibility of cardiac ablation, a procedure that could potentially help manage his arrhythmias more effectively.

During our appointment, the electrophysiologist reviewed Landon's condition and confirmed that, despite the potential to develop supraventricular tachycardia (SVT), he is presently not exhibiting any significant or troubling symptoms that would necessitate immediate intervention.

Instead of surgery, we would continue to monitor his condition.

Whenever he felt unwell, he would inform me so we could document it in his journal for his upcoming doctor visits. His episodes became more frequent, but once he took a moment to relax and sit down, his symptoms would subside. While he managed his unease, it remained a concern for us both.

After consulting two cardiologists and an electrophysiologist, I felt uneasy despite the examinations, echocardiogram, and blood tests. Lying in bed, I considered requesting a stress test for more clarity. The next morning, I called the doctor's office to explain what was still happening—shortness of breath, heart palpitations, dizziness, exertion headaches, and fatigue—urging them to perform a stress test to ensure we have ruled out all possibilities.

The cardiologist agreed to schedule the appointment and suggested consulting a pulmonologist first to rule out exercise-induced asthma, as it could impact the test results. Landon's breathing problems were a concern, and I was determined to explore every option. I felt reassured knowing the medical team genuinely cared about my son's well-being and leading us in the right direction.

Pulmonology Concerns

After returning home from the cardiologist, the weight of uncertainty felt like a heavy blanket around my shoulders. Landon needed a pediatric pulmonologist and finding one covered by our insurance became my immediate mission. I dove into research, sifting through profiles, reviews, and qualifications, determined to make an informed choice for my son. Finally, I chose a pulmonologist whom I instinctively felt would understand Landon's needs.

As we arrived for the appointment, I could sense the anxiety swirling between us. We clearly communicated our concerns to the pulmonologist, who listened intently before performing a thorough examination. The lung function tests that followed were both daunting and enlightening. When the results came back, they were alarming: severe airway obstruction. The doctor acted quickly, ordering a chest X-ray on the spot, and emphasizing the need for comprehensive pulmonary function tests.

That day, as we drove home, I felt my composure beginning to crack. I usually wore my strength like armor, shielding Landon from worry, but the gravity of the situation pressed down on my heart. I took a deep breath, tears flowing down my face like a waterfall. Then I decided it was time to be honest. I turned to him and said, *"I'm so sorry for what you're going through. It breaks my heart to see you facing these challenges. I wish I could take it all away—I would in a second."*

In an unexpected twist, Landon reached out and gently squeezed my hand as he handed me a tissue to wipe my tears *"Mommy, it's okay,"* he said softly. *"We just need to follow the doctors' orders, and we'll figure it out one step at a time, like we always do.*" His words pierced through my worry like a ray of sunlight, filling my heart with overwhelming pride for this remarkable young man. His courage and resilience amidst uncertainty became a beacon of strength for me, reminding me that we were in this together.

The day of Landon's pulmonary function test arrived. I felt empowered but also nauseous. My stomach churned with worries about what the results might reveal. Watching him go through the tests was stressful, especially with the technician's remarks about how Landon's technique might affect his results. Is it his technique, or is he struggling? I wondered.

Some of the tests were particularly challenging and required clear instructions with a visual demonstration, which I did my best to provide. Yet, one test left Landon visibly defeated. He looked at me, eyes filled with both determination and despair, and said, *"I just can't do it."* In that moment, I realized all I could offer was encouragement. *"You've done your best, and that's what matters,"* I assured him.

After the tests, the doctor called to discuss the findings. I felt a flicker of hope when he told me Landon had improved from previous assessments. However, he mentioned a cautionary note: his ongoing symptoms—shortness of breath, dizziness, and headaches during physical activity might be linked to gastrointestinal issues. The doctor suggested monitoring the situation and reaching out if things worsened.

But my instincts screamed that we couldn't afford a wait-and-see approach. I felt an urgent need to investigate further and uncover the root of Landon's symptoms. I told his pulmonologist I planned to consult both his cardiologist and gastroenterologist to discuss potential next steps. I wanted to ensure we were being thorough in seeking a definitive diagnosis.

"I understand your concerns," he said gently. *"To get to the bottom of this, I recommend an exercise stress test. It will help us evaluate his heart and overall fitness under controlled conditions."* I agreed without hesitation before ending the call.

I felt a weight lift from my chest, even with unanswered questions. I was also relieved to learn that his lungs were in good condition, meaning we had one less doctor to see for now.

Stress Test

On the day of the stress test, I felt hopeful and confident that we would find clarity. After checking in, we settled in the waiting area. When his name was called, a friendly nurse led us to the examination room, where the cardiologist greeted us with a reassuring smile. The nurse connected Landon to the heart monitor, revealing that his WPW was very active. His blood pressure was low at 80/60, and the cardiologist asked if this was typical for him, to which I confirmed it had been a concern since his last surgery in June 2024.

The cardiologist asked Landon if he felt strong enough to undergo the stress test. Though I had questions, I held back until Landon responded. He confidently nodded to proceed. As he walked on the treadmill, his blood pressure fluctuated between 90/60 and 110/70. He felt tired and dizzy but insisted on continuing. After the 12-minute test, his blood pressure reading was 98/60. Though dizzy, he wasn't close to fainting but requested to sit down.

Surprisingly, the test results showed that his WPW pattern didn't appear during elevated heart rates, reducing the likelihood of developing supraventricular tachycardia (SVT). This information filled us with great joy and gratitude, as it confirmed that he was considered low risk.

Orthostatic hypotension was a possibility raised by Landon's cardiologist after the test. Intrigued and slightly nervous, we learned that this condition involves significant drops in blood pressure upon standing, which would explain the dizziness he'd been experiencing even without exercise. She recommended increasing his sodium and potassium intake and advised him to follow a structured exercise regimen for the next 30 days to improve his cardiovascular health.

A month later, the day of his follow-up appointment arrived. Landon was anxious but optimistic. The doctor performed a complete orthostatic examination, which included various tests to measure his blood pressure and heart rate. Some results were promising, but others raised concerns. The doctor explained that while some findings were positive, they couldn't yet make an official diagnosis.

"We need to evaluate him over time to ensure we didn't overlook anything," she calmly stated. Although we

left the doctors with an unclear path, we now had clarity on what could be causing his symptoms.

On the drive home, I saw Landon's relief at the progress made, but uncertainty still loomed. He couldn't shake the feeling that he wasn't out of the woods yet. Questions about his health lingered in his mind, and he felt the weight of the unknown. *"When do you think we'll know more? What if they find nothing?"* he hesitantly asked. I reassured him that, with time, we would get the information we needed and that we wouldn't give up until we received answers.

Determined to face whatever lay ahead, we embraced the idea that plans were in motion to tackle the mystery of his health. We committed to his exercise regimen even more fervently, focusing on improving his heart rate, increasing his strength, and taking long walks to clear his mind together. He continued to follow his healthy diet, incorporating electrolyte drinks to ensure his body received the nutrition it needed.

As the weeks passed and follow-up appointments came and went, Landon came to appreciate the importance of patience. There are still many unanswered questions, but he is learning to find peace in the uncertainty.

CHAPTER *7*

One Voice, One Path

The Journey of Advocacy and the IEP Process

As Landon neared his third birthday, I was overwhelmed with anxiety. Transitioning from the services outlined in his Individualized Family Service Plan (IFSP) to our local school district felt like stepping into the unknown, yet I was eager to embrace this new chapter. I hoped this change would be beneficial for him, providing the educational support he needed to thrive. We had worked hard to nurture his growth in his early years, and now it was time to take the next step.

The school district had contacted us about the need for an evaluation for the developmental preschool program. My mind raced as I balanced feelings of hope for Landon's future with the gnawing worry that came with the uncertainty of his eligibility. I knew his eligibility wouldn't depend solely on his diagnosis, leaving room for doubt. Still,

I sensed that if he could gain access to this program, it could open doors to essential resources and opportunities for him.

As the meeting day drew near, I felt a blend of anticipation and apprehension. My understanding of the special education system was still a patchwork quilt of fragmented knowledge, pieced together by my experiences and occasional insights into the process. Despite my efforts to advocate for Landon thus far, I realized I had never faced a full team of experts. The thought of navigating this terrain filled me with anxiety and doubt—could I effectively advocate for Landon in such a crucial setting?

On the day of the IEP meeting, I walked into a room that felt suffocating, weighed down by binders filled with information about Landon's journey. Each binder was packed with notes, evaluations, tests, and reports that chronicled his progress, yet they seemed inadequate to capture the full scope of who he was. Just when I thought I had grasped everything I needed to know, I was bombarded by a whirlwind of new terminology and complex regulations swirling in my mind.

The paradox of feeling prepared yet utterly overwhelmed hit me hard as I took in the scene before me. The conference room was filled with professionals, each equipped with their own expertise and stacks of paperwork.

Names and titles floated over my head like a foreign language, and I felt a lump forming in my throat. I had practiced my points, rehearsed my words, and visualized this moment countless times, but sitting there, I couldn't shake the sense of being an outsider.

As the meeting began, the experts discussed assessments and strategies, occasionally tossing in terms that felt foreign to me. I struggled to keep up, half-listening while mentally calculating how to advocate for Landon in the midst of this whirlwind of expertise. A knot tightened in my stomach, hovering between hope and apprehension.

Then, unexpectedly, a wave of clarity broke through. The case manager paused to ask me about Landon and his interests, pulling me into the conversation. Her question acted as a lifeline. I spoke passionately about his curiosity for dinosaurs, his love for art, his fascination with water—whether in it or near it—and his interest in trains. As I shared, I remembered that beneath the layers of evaluations and qualifications, Landon was still just a little boy with dreams and joys that deserved recognition.

I seized the moment, articulating my hopes for Landon and the kind of support I believed would help him thrive. Each word empowered me, grounding my thoughts in the research I had studied—the late nights learning about special education, and the conversations with other parents who had walked this path before me. I spoke with conviction, detailing not only Landon's challenges but also his incredible strengths—his creativity, his love for exploration, his heart of gold and warm affection, and his potential to excel in the right environment.

When the evaluation results were finally shared, a palpable shift took place in the room. The case worker looked directly at me with a professional yet warm smile. *"Landon qualifies for the preschool disabled program,"* she announced. In that moment, relief swept over me, washing away the doubts and fears I had clung to throughout the meeting.

I could feel the tension release from my shoulders as I looked around the room, meeting the eyes of the professionals who had listened intently. I wanted to jump up, scream, and hug everyone in the room. The news that the district was equipped to meet all of Landon's needs was an immense relief, lifting a weight I hadn't fully realized I was carrying.

Knowing we wouldn't have to navigate the daunting task of seeking out-of-district services, which had seemed overwhelming and intimidating, brought an immense comfort. The thought of sifting through endless options, meeting with unfamiliar faces, and trying to piece together what Landon required had been exhausting.

Now, it felt like a door had swung wide open, revealing a path of support tailored just for him.

As I left the meeting, my binders felt lighter in my hands. Armed with the reassurance that Landon would receive the services and support he needed, I stepped into the future with renewed hope. This wasn't the end—it was the beginning of a partnership built on understanding, support, and the shared goal of helping my son thrive.

With the first step behind us, a world of possibilities stretched before us, bright and inviting. Excitement bubbled within me as I prepared for the journey ahead. My son, Landon, was beginning a new chapter, and with it, the focus shifted to his Individualized Education Plan (IEP).

The day I first sat down with the IEP document remains etched in my memory. The sheer volume of information was overwhelming—a sea of jargon and acronyms that felt insurmountable. Yet, instead of succumbing to discouragement, I took a deep breath and decided to dive in.

His IEP was a roadmap—a comprehensive document outlining his disability, strengths, and weaknesses, along with the accommodations he needed to thrive in school. It was tailored to him, to his journey.

The Individuals with Disabilities Education Act (IDEA) guaranteed him a free public education while emphasizing the importance of learning in a supportive environment. I envisioned him in a classroom where he could connect with peers as his laughter echoed alongside theirs.

Time passed, and just as Landon evolved, so did his IEP. Every year, we revisited its contents, discussing the measurable goals we had set and how he was progressing. We celebrated each triumph—whether big or small—and tackled any challenges with a collaborative spirit. Our team became a united force, committed to providing the best for Landon.

Through meticulous documentation, I began to notice patterns in his development—what worked and what didn't. Each progress report became a window into his journey, detailing his triumphs on one page and moments of difficulty on another. Before meetings, I would compile a list of questions and any new information I had gathered to ensure we made the most of our time together. Each meeting was an opportunity for me to express my thoughts, and I was committed to ensuring that nothing was overlooked.

As each reevaluation drew nearer, a sense of anticipation settled in. Would the current plan still serve him well? Would we need to adjust our strategies? Which classroom setting is best for his development now? As a team, we assessed Landon's current situation and established realistic, actionable goals. The discussions became fluid, less daunting with each passing year.

Over time, I started to view IEP meetings not as a chore but as a valuable opportunity to foster change and growth for Landon. It became a chance for my voice to be heard without judgment or gaslighting. Each time I left the table, I felt a little taller, every inch reflective of the newfound strength I had cultivated in advocating for his well-being and education. The once-daunting road ahead was now adorned with possibilities—a pathway forged by understanding, compassion, and teamwork.

In this ongoing journey, I learned that the true value of an IEP lies not only in its documentation but in the relationships fostered throughout the process. We had become a team, united by our mission: to help Landon navigate his world and thrive within it. And as I looked ahead, I felt gratitude—because the journey was ours, and we were just getting started.

Landon began his first few years in a self-contained classroom, a space vibrant with colors and filled with supportive resources. This was where he felt safe and understood, a sanctuary offering personalized support. Landon wasn't just learning academics; he was also engaging in speech therapy, ABA, and occupational therapy—both in and out of the classroom.

For Landon, the years from Pre-K to second grade were a whirlwind of growth and discovery, a transformative journey that laid the foundation for who he would become. From his very first day in Pre-K, he walked into the classroom with wide eyes, taking in the colorful array of art supplies, toys, and friendly faces.

His teacher had an innate ability to create a nurturing, inclusive atmosphere. She understood that each child in her class was unique, and she took the time to learn what helped each student thrive. For Landon, who sometimes felt overwhelmed by the noise and chaos of classroom life, her gentle encouragement to express his thoughts was like a soft embrace.

Under her guidance, Landon discovered a voice he didn't know he had. Activities that once seemed daunting became opportunities for self-expression. Whether it was sharing his favorite story during circle time or leading a small group project about shapes and colors, he learned to advocate for his ideas. His confidence blossomed, and with each success, his enthusiasm for school grew.

Landon began to flourish in ways I had only hoped for and as Kindergarten approached, he grew excited. It was an environment brimming with potential, and at the heart of it all were his teacher and her devoted aide.

He quickly picked up reading skills, driven by a strong desire to dive into the stories that captivated his imagination. His teachers noticed his passion and introduced him to more complex books, which sparked his love for adventure and knowledge. It was as if they could see the spark within him long before he recognized it himself.

His aide played an equally pivotal role in Landon's journey. With a talent for one-on-one support, she ensured that Landon understood the lessons being taught. When reading and writing seemed too challenging, or science experiments felt overwhelming, she was right there, patiently breaking down concepts and celebrating each small victory. She encouraged him to embrace the learning process with curiosity rather than fear.

Landon's growing sense of security in that nurturing classroom extended beyond academics. With his teacher and aide promoting kindness and friendship, he learned how to connect with his classmates. Group activities became less intimidating, and playtime transformed into opportunities to forge new friendships. They practiced turn-taking and listening—both essential skills that continued to blossom in him.

Before the year ended, I took the time to email the principal to express my gratitude for the staff dedicated to the school and the children. In my message, I highlighted the exceptional qualities of Landon's aide and asked if he would consider allowing her to continue as his aide in the upcoming year.

Unfortunately, my request did not lead to the desired outcome, but the principal acknowledged my heartfelt email and thanked me for my kind words. He explained that, although he wished he could accommodate my request, he could not show favoritism, which I understood.

During first grade, Landon experienced remarkable growth in his early educational journey. He honed his skills in letter formation, mastering the intricacies of writing each letter with precision. His ability to read sight words expanded significantly, boosting his confidence as a budding reader. Throughout these formative years, Landon thrived on the consistency of a structured routine, which gave him a sense of security and stability.

His fascination with learning blossomed as he explored the world around him, especially when discovering the intricacies of animals and the wonders of nature. Math and spelling quickly became his favorite subjects, where numbers and letters transformed into engaging puzzles. He often took the initiative to count everyday objects—whether it was the number of pictures hanging on the wall or the toys scattered across the floor—and delight in spelling their names aloud, showcasing his growing vocabulary and understanding.

Learning became a joyful adventure for Landon, fueling his desire to explore even further. He eagerly looked forward to science projects that offered hands-on experiences, such as crafting colorful slime and creating captivating snow globes. The excitement reached a peak when he engaged in experiments that involved making volcanoes, fully immersing himself in the sensory experience—the eruptions, bubbling sounds, and the vibrant colors all captured his imagination.

Throughout his early years, I watched Landon's world expand in extraordinary ways, filled with curiosity and wonder. Each milestone in his learning brought a new layer of discovery, and I cherished every moment spent together, celebrating his achievements and nurturing his love for knowledge.

As he grew, so did his dreams of independence. He watched his classmates interact during recess, their laughter resonating like melodic birds. With each passing day, Landon's desire to join them grew stronger, but the reliance on his aide sometimes felt like a weight holding him back.

The specialized instruction that had nurtured him started to present challenges. Landon often felt the sting of social isolation, realizing that while his aide provided comfort, it also made him dependent on her for interaction.

One day after school, a pivotal moment arrived. Landon expressed that he no longer needed an aide. He wanted to explore all the avenues of school independently. At first, my immediate reaction was to reject his request, concerned about the challenges he might face without support. But as I looked into his eyes, his confidence began to shift my perspective.

"I'll let you know my decision in a little while after we have a family discussion," I told him. He nodded in agreement, understanding that we needed to weigh this significant change carefully.

During our conversation that evening, Landon shared his feelings. *"My friends always ask why I have a teacher following and helping me,"* he said earnestly. *"I told them I need help sometimes, but I think I can do things on my own now or try."* I could see the determination in his eyes as he continued, *"If I need help, I will ask for it, just like you've taught me. Please, Mommy."*

It struck me then how much he wanted to embrace his independence—to demonstrate that he was capable. How could I say no to that? He was articulating his needs so clearly; who was I to dictate what he needed at this stage in his life? I knew in my heart that he was ready for this leap, and I was beyond proud that he recognized his potential as well.

With a smile on my face, I finally said, *"I'll make the call tomorrow."* The joy on Landon's face was instantaneous. He flapped his hands excitedly, a gesture of pure delight. In an instant, he was up, wrapping his arms around me in a tight hug before darting off to his room to tackle his homework while chanting, *"I'm a big boy."*

As I watched him go, I felt a mix of pride and optimism. This was a significant moment, not just for him, but for all of us. It marked the beginning of another chapter—one where Landon could navigate the world with a little more freedom and autonomy.

The next morning, I spoke with his case manager about what had happened. She was overjoyed to hear about the change and immediately began revising his plan. We revisited his IEP to ensure that, should any challenges arise, a one-on-one aide would be reinstated.

Each week, I worked closely with his teachers and therapists, sharing observations and strategies to support Landon's growth and foster his independence without an aide. The feedback I received from the staff was invaluable, highlighting areas where he was thriving and identifying those that required more time and practice.

Rather than hovering in the background, I cheered him on from a distance, watching with pride as he approached his classmates with growing confidence. It was heartwarming to see him face new challenges with an adventurous spirit, fully embracing his journey both in school and beyond.

At first, there were rumbles of hesitation. Landon stumbled through conversations, his words sometimes tumbling out awkwardly. But with each interaction, he took a step closer to his goal. His classmates began to notice his efforts, inviting him more often to play. With this new encouragement, Landon found himself surrounded by laughter and games, his spirit soaring higher than ever.

He discovered that mistakes were part of learning and that friendships were built on shared experiences. He learned to voice his thoughts, express his feelings, and advocate for himself in ways I hadn't imagined. Each small victory—whether joining a group activity, articulating a new word, or initiating conversations with his peers fortified his growing self-assurance.

By the end of second grade, Landon had cultivated an impressive sense of independence. Gone were the days when he relied on an aide by his side; he had evolved into a self-assured young individual, facing challenges with unwavering determination. He learned to confidently articulate his needs to teachers and peers—skills that became particularly vital as he transitioned to new grade levels.

As Landon navigated the complexities of a larger classroom environment, his growth was nothing short of remarkable. He built meaningful friendships, engaged actively in group activities, and showcased his adventurous spirit and natural curiosity. Each day, he approached learning opportunities with unabated enthusiasm, whether tackling complex math problems or participating in creative arts projects. Even as challenges rose, he found ways to cope with the support of his team.

At one point, however, the vibrant energy of the classroom transformed into a cacophony of noise and activity that overwhelmed Landon. Each day, he confronted a chaotic environment—classmates laughing, shouting, and fidgeting—making it nearly impossible for him to concentrate. His heart would sink as he struggled to keep pace, and the once-joyful love he had for learning began to be overshadowed by frustration.

As the days turned into weeks, Landon mustered the courage to voice his concerns. *"The noise is too much and I can't complete my work,"* he would confide in me, his brow furrowed with distress. I could see the toll this environment was taking on him. The academic workload was intensifying, filled with assignments that seemed to multiply, while he grappled with overstimulation and anxiety. The struggle to navigate his learning environment became increasingly daunting, leaving him trapped in a cycle of stress that dimmed his once-enthusiastic spirit.

In an effort to cope with the challenges he faced, Landon began unconsciously adopting the behaviors of his classmates and creating his own. I frequently received emails or calls about his behavior—mimicking others during lessons, making playful gestures, laughing at inappropriate moments, having increased meltdowns, and joining off-topic discussions.

Rather than fostering genuine connections, his attempts at imitation deepened the distractions surrounding him. The loud laughter and boisterous energy of his classmates, which he had initially thought would help him fit in, became another barrier to his focus and understanding. As he mirrored their behavior, Landon found himself lost in the noise, struggling to keep up with lessons that sped by, further isolating him from the learning experience he once loved. Each time he shifted his focus to emulate others, he distanced himself from his own identity, sinking deeper into confusion and frustration.

Recognizing that Landon needed a more conducive learning environment, I took the initiative to schedule a meeting with his teachers and support staff. With urgency and determination, I shared my observations about Landon's struggles and the potential benefits of a quieter and more structured classroom setting. I emphasized how such an environment could greatly enhance his ability to focus and engage with the material.

After an extensive discussion, we reached a consensus to transition Landon to a different classroom— one designed to minimize distractions and provide a slower-paced learning experience. This new classroom was equipped with tools and strategies tailored to support students who needed extra focus and more time, allowing for a more personalized approach to education.

The transformation in Landon's experience was remarkable. In this calmer setting, he thrived more than he ever had; the quieter atmosphere and preference for front-row seating allowed him to concentrate deeply on lessons. When frustration mounted, he was given a much-needed water break, allowing him to step away and collect his thoughts. When challenges arose, he received personalized, one-on-one attention. The support made the content more accessible and provided a sense of security and belonging.

For years, Landon had benefited from one-on-one Applied Behavioral Analysis (ABA) therapy, which was crucial in helping him navigate challenges until second grade. Although he graduated from intensive therapy, regular check-ins with his ABA therapist continued into fourth grade, ensuring he maintained progress and addressed any emerging obstacles.

By the time Landon completed ABA therapy, he still had access to ongoing support through occupational and speech therapy. This cumulative support provided him with a range of tools and resources to help him navigate the complexities of middle and high school, laying a foundation for both personal growth and academic success.

As Landon progressed, the speech and occupational therapy services he received shifted from individual to group sessions, with the frequency reduced from two sessions to one. These changes reflected his growth and mastery of specific goals, though the option to increase services remained available if needed.

Over time, he transitioned to mainstream classes, and additional services were integrated into his Individualized Education Program (IEP) as he continued to develop.

As 2023 approached, it became clear that Landon needed additional support. We introduced counseling alongside his speech as a co-treatment to address the emotional challenges stemming from his school experiences. The goal was to create a safe space for him to express his feelings and gain a better understanding of social cues. He wanted to learn the subtle distinctions between real friends and those who might hide their true intentions, having been hurt by past bullying.

The counseling sessions became a crucial part of Landon's support system. He learned to articulate his emotions and engage in social interactions with increased confidence and awareness. Together with his counselor, he explored strategies to identify authentic friendships and how to navigate various social situations effectively.

His success in mainstream classes with fewer accomodations was nothing short of remarkable and truly inspiring. His progress demonstrated not only his resilience but also the effectiveness of the supportive learning environment. Watching him grow was empowering—he no longer felt lost in a sea of social interactions but began to find solid ground.

As each school year ended and a new one began, I found myself eagerly anticipating an important milestone in Landon's educational journey: his first IEP meeting. It was a moment I had long prepared for, filled with both excitement and apprehension. I knew that discussing his strengths, areas for growth, and goals for the year could be overwhelming, given the volume of information we needed to cover and the weight of the conversation focusing solely on him.

Over the years, I had gradually introduced the concept of these meetings to Landon in a way that made sense to him. *"Imagine,"* I told him, *"We're all in a room together—your teachers, therapists, case manager, guidance counselor, and your family—talking about how well you're doing in school and how we can help you succeed.*"

I stressed that the meeting wasn't just about checking boxes; it was about understanding what truly helped him thrive, whether it was specific study techniques, test-taking strategies, or ways to reduce distractions in the classroom.

Landon and I discussed the challenges he faced at school—how certain subjects were more difficult than others and how, at times, he needed additional support to navigate social interactions. It was crucial for him to understand that his voice mattered and that learning to advocate for himself would be an invaluable skill as he grew older.

He expressed confidence in his ability to make decisions about his life while also asking me to be by his side for guidance when needed. In that moment, I felt a mix of pride and gratitude, watching him prepare to take an active role in his educational journey. After years of advocating for him, I realized he wasn't just absorbing information; he was learning to fight for his own needs and aspirations, and his determination was evident in every small victory.

When we attended our first meeting with the school district's Child Study Team, I was deeply impressed by the genuine care and attentiveness they showed toward Landon, as though they were meeting him for the first time. They were so engaged, listening carefully as he spoke and asking insightful questions to ensure they understood his perspective. Their dedication to fostering his academic success and well-being reassured me of the reasons we'd stayed in this school district since he was three years old.

I felt an overwhelming sense of gratitude for the exceptional professionals we've had the privilege to work with. From the dedicated educators to the therapists, coaches, and supportive aides and bus drivers who have all played a crucial role in Landon's growth. It's heartwarming to see how much they care.

Whether it was a heartfelt gesture, a word of encouragement spoken at just the right moment, a safe ride to school, a lesson expertly taught with patience and care, or a therapeutic session that offered a safe space for expression and development, each of these actions held profound significance. The commitment of those around us truly transformed his life and shaped our journey as a family. With only one path laid out before us, we united in following the one voice that guided our way forward: Landon.

CHAPTER *8*

~~~~~~~~~~~~~~

Holding onto to Hope Through Treatment

As we began developing Landon's treatment plan, the path ahead felt daunting, but full of promise. My days were consumed with research—pouring over books, articles, and connecting with professionals who could offer insight into the most effective therapies and treatments. Every step was aimed at empowering Landon, not just to navigate daily life, but to learn how to manage the behaviors that sometimes held him back.

From the very beginning, my primary focus was to understand and connect with Landon on a level beyond words. Before he could express his needs, I observed his responses to the world around him, interpreting his thoughts, cues, and emotions to help him. I found strength in his affection, laughter, curiosity, and the unique ways he expressed joy. It became clear that Landon had his distinct strengths and talents—qualities I recognized as the foundation upon which we would build.

I explored a variety of services designed specifically for him. I contacted therapists in different fields, toured therapy centers, bought specialized tools and equipment, created routines, and researched dietary changes and necessary supplements. I immersed myself in understanding each one's potential impact, from communication-aiding technology devices to interventions that enhanced social skills. Each new piece of information felt like a puzzle fitting into place.

Throughout this process, I prioritized staying open-minded. Every question I asked and every conversation I had—whether with doctors, educators, or fellow parents unveiled new insights into Landon's needs. I discovered that the more I explored, the more answers I uncovered, often leading to better outcomes and adjustments in our approach.

Our journey, while undeniably challenging, has also been a testament to resilience, patience, and hope. The services that supported Landon continue to bring about profound changes, reshaping his abilities and transforming our lives together.

As I share our experiences, I hope others can find inspiration and encouragement in them. With dedication, love, and a willingness to adapt, we can all support our children's development, ensuring they have the resources to navigate their paths confidently and joyfully. And while Landon's journey is far from over, I believe that with every step forward, we are creating a brighter future filled with possibilities.

Applied Behavioral Analysis (ABA)

Landon, a bright and curious boy with big dreams and an endless sense of wonder often faced a world that felt overwhelming. At just three years old, his unique way of understanding and engaging with his environment became evident. He often struggled with adapting to daily changes, leading to moments of frustration that could dim his radiance.

Noticing his challenges, I sought help through the local school system, believing that Applied Behavioral Analysis (ABA) therapy could provide the support Landon needed to thrive. I envisioned a future where he could communicate effectively, build social skills, adapt to change, and feel confident in his daily activities. But when we attended the evaluation meeting, our hopes were dashed—a denial letter arrived, stating that Landon's needs weren't considered severe enough to qualify for the services he truly needed.

Disheartened, I couldn't understand how the decision had been made. Despite Landon's formal diagnosis and comprehensive reports from his neurologist, my concerns were dismissed, and the school district insisted that the care they offered was sufficient. Driven by a fierce love for my son, I began researching the ins and outs of special education, focusing on its laws and funding.

Through research, I uncovered the complexities schools face due to limited resources and funding. I learned that when government grants expire, schools often had to make tough choices, which, unfortunately, meant children like Landon sometimes fell through the cracks.

As anger bubbled inside me, I decided to reach out to several attorneys. I gathered a mountain of paperwork in preparation for an appeal or lawsuit. Then, out of the blue, life threw a curveball: we had to relocate due to an unfortunate situation. Instead of feeling defeated, I recognized this as a blessing in disguise. With renewed hope, I paused our search for legal support and chose to explore what the new school district could offer.

Settling into our new home was comforting and provided me with the time I needed to prepare for our meeting with the child study team. When the day finally arrived, I felt anxious. I was sweating, my hands were shaking, my head ached, and my heart raced. I had spent months getting ready for the day he would start school, and as I approached the door and rang the bell to enter, it felt as though I was losing everything I once knew.

To my surprise, the school radiated warmth and understanding—a place that valued every child's potential. The staff embraced Landon's individuality, eager to provide the one-on-one assistance and ABA therapy he truly needed. There was no pushback. This school was committed to nurturing students of all abilities, ensuring Landon's strengths were recognized and his challenges addressed.

Landon's first day of school is a memorable moment. Although anxiety gripped him, he excitedly walked through the doors with his Thomas the Train backpack, looking back with a smile and waving.

As Landon settled into his new environment, his teachers noticed that transitions and changes in routine led to behavioral difficulties for him. When overwhelmed, he would collapse on the floor or stiffen his body, signaling his need for support. To help him adjust more smoothly, they introduced a three-stage visual timetable that outlined past, present, and future tasks and activities. This simple yet effective tool helped Landon better understand his day and anticipate changes, alleviating some of his anxiety and frustration.

His teachers and therapists recognized his love for trains, but they also noticed that he sometimes struggled with transitions and maintaining focus on other activities. To help him adapt, his ABA (Applied Behavior Analysis) therapist implemented strategies to nurture his skills. She concentrated on key areas, such as taking turns, engaging with various toys and interactive play, creating a visual chart of coping mechanisms, and ensuring smooth and safe transitions between activities.

One day, the teachers introduced a schedule that included an allotted time for train play, but with a twist. They explained that after train time, they would dive into a range of activities—coloring, reading, board games, dancing, and even building with blocks or LEGO. At first, Landon struggled to accept the time limits on his beloved trains. He expressed his frustration, not quite understanding why he had to put them away.

However, as days turned into weeks, something remarkable happened. With the help of his teachers and therapists, Landon began to adapt to the routine and opening up to new ideas. He discovered that trying out new activities was just as fun and engaging. He started to request different toys and activities, shifting away from his singular focus on trains. His creativity blossomed as he painted colorful pictures, constructed amazing LEGO towers, and enjoyed outdoor adventures.

But the journey wasn't without its challenges. Landon sometimes called out in class, tapped his pencil, and giggled at inappropriate times, often as a response to his sensory needs. His teachers closely observed these behaviors, gaining insight into the links between his actions and sensory experiences. They realized that what seemed like attention-seeking was also Landon's way of coping with changes and engaging with his environment.

A star reward chart was introduced by his team to provide Landon with additional support. He could earn stars for each positive behavior, motivating him to engage in constructive actions throughout the day. Although the system worked wonders initially, it wasn't long before Landon became overly focused on collecting stars, rather than on the underlying behaviors that truly mattered.

Determined to help him succeed, his teacher introduced a traffic light behavior program. This tool featured a vibrant green, yellow, and red light, each color representing a different level of behavior. Green meant he was doing great; yellow signified that he needed a gentle reminder to refocus, and red indicated that he had strayed off task.

His teacher made it a point to ensure that the traffic light system was clear and engaging. Whenever Landon needed a reminder, she would quietly give him up to three warnings before discreetly changing the color of the traffic light. At first, Landon was nervous about being called out for his behavior, but the teacher's gentle approach made it easier for him to accept the changes.

When Landon got back on track within six to ten minutes after a color change, his teacher would change it. She would praise him for his efforts, saying, *"I saw you focused on your work! Great job!"* This recognition made Landon feel proud and appreciated that even when he faltered, the spotlight wasn't always on him.

The efforts didn't stop there. His teacher, who had Landon for several years in elementary school, implemented systems like Class Cash and Class Dojo, where his positive behaviors were reinforced and rewarded. She understood Landon very well and never stopped trying to find ways to help him.

He participated in 30-minute sessions of ABA every day during preschool, but as he moved on to kindergarten through second grade, those sessions increased to 60 minutes daily. The longer days brought new routines, challenges, and expectations. At times, he found it difficult to manage the longer sessions and the increasing workload, leading to meltdowns and resistance.

During these moments, his teachers and therapist recognized the need to adapt to Landon's needs. Some days, they concluded sessions early, allowing him time to relax and regain his composure. Initially, I worried that cutting the sessions might hinder Landon's progress. But I soon realized that pushing him too hard would only heighten his stress.

Landon's heightened sensory often made engaging with his lessons difficult. By giving him space when he felt overwhelmed, he was able to process his emotions more effectively. In the calming moments that followed, he discovered coping techniques: deep breaths, counting to ten, communicating his feelings, and asking for breaks when needed.

With each passing day, Landon became more adept at managing his emotions. Whenever he faced new challenges, he felt equipped to think through solutions rather than react impulsively. Over time, Landon blossomed into a thoughtful and resilient learner, proving to himself that he could tackle anything that came his way.

By the time Landon reached third grade, he had entered a new chapter in his educational journey. He transitioned from an intensive support model to a more nurturing environment. With weekly check-ins, his teachers and therapists ensured he could apply the strategies he had learned during his ABA therapy in a more dynamic classroom setting.

These weekly sessions became a cornerstone of his development. He learned to integrate the tactics from his therapy into everyday activities, transforming lessons into exciting challenges rather than overwhelming obstacles. Fourth grade brought new opportunities, and Landon continued to thrive on this supportive path, steadily incorporating his learning strategies into his school days.

From his earliest days in preschool through extended school year program during the summer, Landon worked diligently to reshape his behavior management into a powerful tool for learning. He learned to express his needs clearly and effectively, leaving behind the days when he would resort to negative behaviors.

By the end of fourth grade, his remarkable progress was undeniable. He had developed a self-sustaining strategy that not only guided him but also marked a significant milestone—he no longer needed ABA services. This moment felt like winning a hard-fought race, a testament to his personal and academic growth.

His therapist played an essential role in this process, offering insightful feedback and support. Together with his teachers, they broke his overarching goals into manageable phases, instilling a sense of courage and purpose within him. They equipped him with vital coping mechanisms, helping him navigate the often-overwhelming waters of sensory overload and frustration.

While life had its tough moments, Landon learned to listen to his body and mind. He discovered that it was okay to take a step back instead of pushing through discomfort. Everyone encouraged him to speak up, seek help when needed, and prioritize his well-being. With the support of his family, teachers, therapists, and friends, Landon continues to venture into the world, eager to spread his wings and fly.

Occupational Therapy (OT)

At just 2 years old, when I learned that Landon's early intervention application for occupational therapy had been denied, I was determined to find another way for him to thrive. With funding through private insurance, we arranged for twenty therapy sessions per year, starting with twice-weekly appointments. However, the costs quickly became overwhelming. Before long, we had to shoulder the full expense, forcing us to cut his sessions to once every two weeks until the new calendar year, when insurance benefits would reset.

Despite these challenges, a silver lining appeared— just before Landon turned three, he finally qualified for OT through early intervention. Due to the limited availability of therapists, he was able to participate in only a few sessions before the school district took over, allowing him to resume twice-weekly sessions. The frequency of his sessions fluctuated depending on his progress, but having consistent support made all the difference. His journey was anything but straightforward. It was a process of trial and error, carefully figuring out which approaches worked best for him.

In 2010, during his initial preschool evaluation, Landon's friendly nature shone through. His eagerness to participate was heartwarming, yet the evaluators noticed that he sometimes became overwhelmed and needed regular breaks to refocus. They observed that his motor skills were developing at a level similar to children aged 13 to 35 months. While his low muscle tone occasionally made him appear clumsy, it was clear that—with the right support—he had a path forward.

The evaluation also showed that Landon was still determining his hand dominance. His grip on writing tools was evolving, shifting from a clumsy, childlike hold to a more controlled fist. Simple tasks, like molding playdough into shapes or cutting paper with scissors, proved difficult. These struggles highlighted areas where he needed extra support, shaping the structure of his therapy sessions to refine his motor skills while nurturing his love for play.

Landon's heart brimmed with curiosity, but fear often held him back—fear of getting hurt, fear of failing, fear of not doing things perfectly. His occupational therapist recognized these challenges and worked closely with him, setting specific goals to help him push through his hesitations. Progress came in waves. Some days, he took steps forward. Other days, it felt like skills he had mastered were slipping away. It was a winding road, riddled with frustrations, but he pressed on.

Through every struggle, Landon's determination never wavered. His resilience was nothing short of inspiring. Whether he was cutting paper into shapes or daring to try a new activity, he was learning more than just motor skills— he was learning to believe in himself.

In 2012, Landon's hand dominance became evident. His right hand moved with purpose, expertly wielding scissors as he tackled craft projects with enthusiasm. Meanwhile, his left hand played a supportive role, steadying the paper while his mind buzzed with creativity.

Though he loved to color, his wrist sometimes faltered, making it difficult to keep crayons within the lines. Yet, what he lacked in coordination, he made up for with a remarkable talent for spotting hidden images in puzzles and pictures. This skill became his anchor, helping him navigate the daily challenges he encountered.

With focused occupational therapy, Landon made steady progress. He strengthened his core, refined his motor skills, explored his sensory needs, and developed an organizational system tailored to his needs. As he grew, we remained vigilant, knowing that high school would bring a new set of challenges. Anticipating the transition, we set fresh, targeted goals to help him adapt to a more demanding and complex environment.

The first year of high school arrived with its own hurdles. The vast layout of the school and the rush of students in the hallways overwhelmed him, triggering anxiety about making it to class on time. Fortunately, his teachers were patient and understanding, recognizing that everyone was adjusting to the new demands. Their kindness eased his worries, allowing him to find his rhythm.

By sophomore year, a remarkable transformation unfolded. Landon embraced self-reliance, managing his schedule meticulously, navigating his school email with confidence, and submitting assignments promptly. He grew bolder, learning to advocate for himself and tackle challenges head-on, applying the skills he had learned in therapy.

However, junior year presented new obstacles. Mainstream classes meant larger groups, noisier environments, and heavier workloads—all significant adjustments. Yet, through determination and resilience, Landon adapted pretty quickly.

His teachers often praised his curiosity, respectfulness and dedication, noting his ability to stay focused despite distractions and his willingness to help others, even when he needed the help. Each compliment filled me with pride, reaffirming how far he had come.

As a senior, Landon continues to attend occupational therapy once a week. Each session focuses on skills he has already mastered while introducing new goals. His therapist adjusts strategies as Landon faces new challenges. Although familiar situations still make him uneasy—such as meeting new people, missing assignments due to absences, and learning new tasks—he has learned to manage his anxiety, proving that growth is a continuous journey.

He embraced a mindset of self-improvement, valuing personal growth over competition. Understanding that true success came from striving to be his best, he approached high school not just as a student but as someone committed to his own development.

Through challenges and triumphs, Landon emerged not just ready for graduation but equipped with life skills that would carry him forward. His resilience and growth became an inspiration—not just to his teachers and peers but to himself as he steps boldly into the future.

Speech Therapy

At nine months old, Landon took his first step into language, joyfully uttering his first word—*"Mama."* It was a magical moment, filling me with excitement for all the conversations that lay ahead. Over the next few months, his words flowed effortlessly, each new sound a delightful surprise. I cheered him on with every milestone, imagining the stories we would one day share.

But as Landon approached thirteen months, his progress suddenly stalled. The lively chatter that once filled our home faded, replaced by cries of frustration and an unsettling silence where words should have been. Concern weighed on me as I watched my sweet boy struggle to express his thoughts and needs. I knew I had to act.

By 2 years old, Landon was enrolled in a speech therapy program, in addition to early intervention, hoping it would help restore his lost language skills. Each session was filled with heartfelt efforts to support his communication, but as the weeks passed, his speech remained limited and unclear. At times, the helplessness was overwhelming.

When the insurance-covered sessions ran out, the expense became ours. Although we reduced the number of sessions, we didn't slow down; instead, we doubled our efforts. Every day became an opportunity to engage Landon in creative and educational ways. We filled our time with vibrant activities—watching educational videos, coloring, reading, attending library activities, writing sight words, and playing games like Simon Says, POP, Hedbanz, and memory matching. Each laugh, each small success, reinforced not just his learning but also the unbreakable bond we shared.

Books were treasures in our home. I read aloud, encouraging Landon to point at pictures and words, mimicking sounds, and phrases. To spark his creativity and engage his senses, we immersed ourselves in block-stacking adventures and sensory play—running our fingers through rice, fingerpainting, exploring different textures inside and outside, and turning everyday moments into fun, educational experiences.

Recognizing the importance of social skills, I planned regular outings to the library, park, zoo, local events in town, and signed him up for age appropriate sports. I wanted to create an environment that nurtured his language development, motor skills, sensory, and social confidence.

Yet, the journey wasn't without hurdles. Some days were filled with frustration, leading to intense outbursts. At times, I found myself giving in, my heart aching at the sight of his distress. But over time, I realized that guiding him through those moments—rather than rescuing him from them—was crucial. I had to strike a delicate balance between compassion and discipline, helping him understand that communication, like any skill, required effort.

Walking this tightrope often left me battling guilt. Was I being too firm? Too soft? But deep down, I knew that excessive gentleness could slow his progress. If I was truly committed to his growth, I had to balance my approach, trusting that small steps would lead to big strides.

After Landon lost his speech, we had to find new ways to communicate. Picture cards, sight words, and simple signs became our lifeline, helping us bridge the gap between thought and expression. We dove into learning as many signs as possible, practicing them at home and in the community. Landon pointed to everyday objects, using signs whenever he could—putting in so much effort to make himself understood. He learned to sign words like more, please, thank you, bottle, sleep, play, swing, eat, help, all done, and bath.

Before his speech returned, these alternative methods of communication became more than just tools—they became a bond. Every gesture, every sign was a bridge between us, built on love and understanding. It was through these moments that I realized communication wasn't just about words; it was about intent, connection, and emotion.

Grocery shopping became an adventure for Landon and me—one that was more than just a routine errand. It was

an extension of our speech sessions at home, turning everyday tasks into moments of learning, joy, and connection. As we stepped into the store's colorful aisles, Landon's eyes sparkled with excitement. He dashed ahead, scanning the shelves with wonder, as though each item held a secret waiting to be discovered.

One afternoon, in the snack aisle, Landon's face lit up as he spotted his favorite cookies. *"Yum!"* he exclaimed, licking his lips and rubbing his belly. Clutching the box tightly, he rushed back to me, his excitement nearly overflowing. *"Yips!"* he shouted, mispronouncing the name, but his joy was contagious. I knelt down, meeting his gaze, savoring the moment. *"Your favorite cookies Chips Ahoy! You want one?"* His eager nod and wide grin filled the air with energy.

Even when he struggled with pronunciation, I made sure to model the correct words without correcting him outright. I wanted to encourage his efforts, trusting that, in time, he would get it right.

With each shopping trip, I noticed Landon still faced challenges with articulation and vocal tone. Sometimes, he struggled to express himself clearly, and misunderstandings became part of our routine. I recalled one moment vividly—I had told him to "put on his shoes quickly because we had to run." Taking my words literally, he hurried to put on his sneakers, ready for a jog. That small misunderstanding became a teaching moment, showing me how important clear communication was in his learning process.

Landon's language journey came with many hurdles—grasping figurative speech, picking up on social cues, and staying focused in conversation. When I used an idiom or a sarcastic remark, he often paused, his puzzled expression asking for an explanation. Though keeping his train of thought wasn't always easy, every breakthrough felt like a victory, another step forward in our grocery store adventures.

As we left the store that day, our cart filled with groceries, I couldn't help but reflect on how far he had come. Each trip was about more than food—it was about learning and building his confidence. Landon's progress was paving the way for the social interactions he longed for, and with every small success, I knew we were moving closer to that goal.

Though he may not yet grasp every idiom or sarcastic remark, his progress is undeniable. His ability to engage in conversations has strengthened, his pronunciation has become clearer, and he now expresses his thoughts and needs with growing confidence. Each speech therapist he has worked with has played a vital role in his journey, making him feel seen, heard, and understood. Their dedication has fueled his development, as they crafted personalized strategies to support his growth.

Over the years, the number of his therapy sessions has varied—some weeks included as many as five, while others had only two—mirroring the ebb and flow of his progress. What began as one-on-one sessions eventually evolved into a dynamic group setting, where he learned not just from his therapists but also from his peers.

With every lesson and each passing year, he continues to grow into a more articulate and self-assured speaker—a testament to the power of patience, support, and his unwavering determination.

Social Skills Groups

From a young age, Landon had a unique spirit—his big brown eyes sparkled with curiosity, yet there was always a hint of hesitation when it came to engaging with his peers. At the park, he often chose to observe rather than dive into the excitement around him. I understood how crucial social skills were for a child's development, but financial challenges made access to structured therapy seem out of reach. Without insurance to cover social skills programs, I felt the weight of uncertainty pressing down on me.

One afternoon at the local library, while flipping through a community newsletter, I came across a listing for "Mommy and Me" classes at a local facility. The program promised to nurture cooperation, fun, play, communication, and problem-solving skills in young children. Hope stirred in me, though I couldn't shake my doubts about whether it would truly make a difference. Still, I enrolled Landon, clinging to the possibility that this could be a turning point.

On the first day, as we stepped into the brightly colored room, Landon clung to my leg, his anxiety palpable. The chatter of children and the hum of cheerful music filled the air, but he hesitated, his small fingers tightening around my hand. Then, the class began—songs, games, dance, playing instruments, and gentle encouragement from a warm, engaging instructor. Slowly, something shifted. The children built towers together, took turns rolling vibrant balls, and learned to share. Bit by bit, Landon inched forward, his confidence flickering to life. He asked for turns, navigated small disagreements, and even laughed when the blocks tumbled down.

Week by week, I watched him blossom. What started as quiet participation grew into eager engagement. He looked forward to each session, drawn in by the supportive atmosphere created by the instructor and fellow parents. With every class, he strengthened his ability to connect with others, learning the rhythm of conversation, the power of teamwork, and, most importantly, the reassuring truth that he wasn't alone in his feelings of uncertainty.

At home, I noticed remarkable changes. Landon became more eager to invite friends over, attend playdates, and even initiate conversations with the neighborhood kids. The fears of judgment that once overshadowed his longing for connection began to fade, replaced by genuine and rewarding friendships.

Still, some challenges remained. He occasionally retreated into his shell, especially in larger groups or unfamiliar settings. At times, he expressed fears of being teased or feeling inadequate. But I continued to encourage him, reinforcing the skills he had learned through the years. Slowly, he gained the confidence to move through these moments of doubt.

One sunny afternoon at the park, I witnessed a heartwarming breakthrough. Landon approached a group of kids playing on the slide. With a gentle nudge, he took a deep breath and asked if he could join. To his surprise, the children welcomed him without hesitation. Before long, he was laughing and running alongside them, basking in a sense of belonging.

I like to believe this moment taught him that building connections takes patience, understanding, and a little bravery. Each shared experience reinforced that everyone connects in their own way—through laughter, quiet companionship, or simple acts of kindness. The supportive adults in his life had shown him the power of uplifting relationships, inspiring him to seek out those who encouraged him rather than those who brought negativity.

In time, Landon gained more than just friends; he developed a deeper understanding of himself. He realized relationships could flourish in many forms—whether through deep, meaningful bonds with a few or in the joyful chaos of a wider circle.

Ultimately, Landon's time in the "Mommy and Me" classes was nothing short of transformative. It opened a door to a world where laughter echoed, friendships grew, and acceptance thrived. With the right guidance and a nurturing environment, he flourished socially, proving that every child has the potential to connect, grow, and shine in their own unique way. And with each step forward, Landon wasn't just shaping his own path—he was paving the way for other children who longed for the same meaningful connections.

Feeding Therapy

From an early age, Landon had a complicated relationship with food. While other children eagerly devoured their meals, he often struggled. He would pocket food in his mouth without swallowing. Certain tastes, textures, and temperatures made him hesitant, and allergies combined with reflux turned mealtimes into a source of anxiety rather than enjoyment.

At nearly 3 years old, I sought out a feeding therapist to help him navigate these challenges. Our journey introduced us to new strategies that slowly transformed eating into a more inviting experience. With patience and understanding, the therapist worked closely with Landon, helping him articulate his preferences and fears around food.

After several productive sessions, the therapist recommended speech therapy as the most effective solution for his feeding difficulties. Brimming with ideas, she outlined small but impactful adjustments we could make at home, along with measurable goals that could be incorporated into his structured plan. The goals crafted would not only address his feeding issues but also foster a healthier, more positive relationship with food.

Landon's world transformed as weeks turned into months and months into years. With consistent support from his therapist and the love and encouragement he received at home and school, he gradually expanded his palate. No longer did he shy away from textures that once unsettled him; instead, he began experimenting with new foods, finding joy in the crunch of fresh apples and the smoothness of mashed potatoes. Food pocketing faded until it became a thing of the past, and mealtimes shifted from moments of hesitation to him eagerly asking for seconds.

His journey, however, was not without its challenges. As he grew, his preferences changed, and his sensory needs evolved in different ways. Yet, he approached each meal with newfound enthusiasm, embracing the careful monitoring we put in place to keep him safe and healthy. With guidance, he learned to read labels and make informed choices, gradually taking charge of his nutritional habits.

Several years later, Landon underwent a remarkable transformation. What had once been a battle with junk food evolved into a passion for wholesome eating. With every colorful plate he prepared, he took another step toward nourishing his body with better choices, consciously shifting away from unhealthy snacks. His dedication to fostering a healthy relationship with food was truly commendable, a reflection of his inner strength.

Now, as he sits down to a beautifully arranged plate of grilled chicken, steamed broccoli, fresh salad, kimchi, and fragrant quinoa or farro, he smiles with genuine pleasure. He has learned not just to eat but to appreciate food in all its forms.

Each bite he takes is more than just a meal—it's a celebration of his journey. A journey filled with ups and downs, hard work, and ultimately, triumph. Landon has truly turned a corner, embracing food not as a foe, but as a friend.

Counseling

In 2023, Landon faced some of his most difficult challenges as he navigated the tumultuous world of adolescence. Bright and introspective, he found himself increasingly weighed down by the relentless negativity at school. Prank calls disrupted his nights, cameras were shoved in his face, and cruel laughter followed him through the hallways. The whispers in classrooms cut deeper than words, turning what should have been a place of learning into a battlefield. Dismissive glances from peers made him feel invisible. Bullying—both subtle and overt—became a harsh reality, leaving him isolated and struggling for acceptance and understanding.

The road was already rough, but nothing could have prepared us for the sudden sinkhole—a moment that felt like the ground caving beneath us. It began with an act of bullying that escalated into a serious situation, one that led to a criminal case. It tested Landon's resilience and pushed my patience to the brink.

As rage and despair threatened to consume me, I found the strength to fight for my son, who had endured far too much. I refused to be a bystander. I organized meetings with school officials, spoke with parents, and sought legal counsel. This wasn't just about bullying anymore; it was about justice, about standing up for basic human rights.

Every setback only fueled my determination. I still remember the court hearing—how my nerves buzzed with adrenaline, how every word carried the weight of our fight. It was never about winning or losing. It was about making sure my son's voice was heard through me.

Slowly, change began to take shape. Conversations were initiated, policies were examined, additional support was implemented, showing us that we weren't alone in this battle. By the case's conclusion, I had already won in my heart and in my son's eyes. Though battered, we were unbroken, carrying our lessons forward into a future that felt brighter than before. We found our way back to the light, but not without moments of darkness.

One evening, after yet another difficult day at school, Landon and I sat together in the quiet of our home. The warm glow of the lamp cast soft shadows on the walls, illuminating his thoughtful expression. I could see the weight of it all pressing down on him, and it pulled at my heart.

"I think I need help," he finally said, his voice steady but tinged with vulnerability.

Those words changed everything.

That night marked a turning point, not just for him but for both of us. Landon made the courageous decision to seek counseling—a choice that filled me with both concern and pride. I saw the toll bullying had taken on his mental health, but more importantly, I saw his strength in facing it head-on.

As I sat next to him on the couch, I placed my hand on his shoulder. *"I'm really proud of you for recognizing that you need support. It takes a lot of strength to face your struggles and embrace this new chapter in your life."* My words came from a place of love and understanding; I wanted him to feel safe.

Landon looked up at me with his big, earnest eyes, seeking both reassurance and understanding. *"I know I have you, Mommy,"* he said quietly, *"but I feel like I need someone else to help me too."* I nodded, fully understanding his need for additional support. It was a brave choice to seek help beyond our family. *"Of course, we can find someone together,"* I replied, wrapping him in a comforting hug. *"I'll always be here for you, no matter what."* I wanted him to know that he wasn't alone in this process and that he had my unwavering support.

Before we began our search, he looked up at me with a hint of worry. *"Mommy, will you be there with me too?"* His question struck me, revealing both his vulnerability and his trust in me. I felt a rush of warmth at the sincerity of his request. *"Absolutely, you never have to ask that,"* I reassured him, my heart swelling with love. *"I'll be right there with you every step of the way."*

As he began his sessions, I saw how counseling opened up new opportunities for Landon. It provided him with tools to better understand and express his emotions. *"Counseling isn't just about talking,"* he explained to me one day. *"It's about learning how to handle tough times and understanding why I feel the way I do."* His willingness to engage in this process reflected his desire for personal growth, and I felt a sense of hope bloom inside me.

Despite the challenges of these experiences, my commitment to supporting Landon never wavered. We talked about everything, turning our conversations into moments of connection where he could share his feelings without fear. My attentiveness to his social media activity helped us address issues promptly when they arose, and slowly, he began to navigate the anxiety and helplessness that had once overwhelmed him.

The turning point came when Landon fully embraced his counseling sessions. As he dove into discussions about emotions, coping strategies, and the power of positive thinking, I saw him start to change. He learned to articulate his feelings, using techniques like deep breathing and positive affirmations. "*I can choose how I respond to what's happening around me,*" he said one day, a newfound confidence shining in his eyes.

With each session, Landon's self-awareness deepened. He was learning not just who he was, but why he thought and felt the way he did. He began to make choices that reflected his worth—choosing friends who respected him and cultivating relationships that brought him joy. It was incredibly rewarding to witness him form connections that provided him with a support system, reminding him that he wasn't alone in his experiences.

As weeks turned into months, Landon's progress became increasingly clear. He walked taller, spoke more openly, and faced challenges with resilience. He began to believe that he deserved happiness, and that belief alone became a powerful motivator for him. The skills he learned in counseling weren't just tools for managing anxiety—they became a foundation for his future.

Watching Landon embrace his journey of self-discovery has been rewarding beyond measure. Each day, he surprises me with his insights, kindness, and the inner strength he has cultivated. I remain committed to supporting him, encouraged by the resilience he has shown and the hope that now fills his future.

In Landon's decision to seek help, he discovered not only how to cope with adversity but also how to thrive in the face of it. As he continues on this path, I'm excited to see where his newfound strength will take him next.

Cognitive Behavioral Therapy

Alongside traditional counseling, Landon embraced Cognitive Behavioral Therapy (CBT), which transformed the way he faced challenges. This method provided him with powerful tools to manage his anxiety and boost his self-esteem.

Through CBT, he learned how his thoughts, emotions, and behaviors are interconnected. It became a turning point in his life, allowing him to identify and challenge the negative thoughts that often clouded his judgment. No longer a prisoner of his past, he began reshaping his perspectives, empowering himself to approach situations with newfound resilience.

He practiced techniques like goal setting and cognitive restructuring, helping him gain clarity about his feelings and actions. By identifying his triggers, he developed healthier coping strategies that improved his confidence, not only in academics but also in social situations and sports like bowling. His commitment to therapy led to significant progress—he felt a profound shift within himself.

Through this journey, Landon cultivated a loving relationship with himself, acknowledging that his feelings and thoughts are valid, even when they are negative. He understands that to overcome this mindset, he needs to talk things through, whether with me, himself, or someone else. The black-and-white thinking that once dominated him began to fade, revealing a spectrum of self-acceptance and understanding. His transformation is inspiring because each day, he is becoming someone who embraces every aspect of who he is.

Witnessing Landon's journey toward confidence, self-love, and self-acceptance inspired me to reflect on my own path. His story reached far beyond the bowling alley, good grades, mastering skills, or navigating difficult relationships. It became a testament to the power we all have within to face our fears, heal from past trauma, and embrace the love that resides in our hearts.

CHAPTER *9*

From Struggles to Strength

Coping with the Unknown

Receiving an autism diagnosis was an overwhelming experience—relieving, scary, shocking, disorienting, and emotionally exhausting. I remember the day everything began to shift. My son, Landon, had always danced to his own rhythm, but by thirteen months, worry began to take root. While other toddlers engaged in play and shared their thoughts with ease, Landon seemed lost in his own world— captivated by the drip of water from the faucet, the way wheels spun on a chair, car, truck, or train, or the intricate patterns of his toys.

One evening, while we danced in the living room, I watched him flap his hands gently, like a bird in flight. Something stirred in me. As I began researching his unique movements and stumbled across autism, a chill ran through me. Questions swarmed my mind: Is something wrong with him? With me? Am I overreacting? How do I stop him from flapping? I pushed those thoughts aside—retreating into denial for a split second until I couldn't anymore.

As weeks turned into months, I kept my fears to myself. It felt like I was walking through fog, carrying the weight of what I didn't yet understand. I was afraid—afraid that Landon might live in a world that wouldn't make room for him, and that I might not be enough to help him find his place in it.

When the neurologist confirmed my suspicions, it felt like an avalanche had crashed down on me—but strangely, it also felt like winning the lottery. Sitting in that sterile office, trying to absorb the words, I realized part of me had already known. Still, hearing the official diagnosis— Autism Spectrum Disorder—felt different. Final. It echoed in my mind like a bell I couldn't unring.

It was like standing on the edge of a cliff, staring into an unknown abyss. I didn't know how deep it was—but I jumped because I had no other choice.

In the days that followed, I became a storm of emotion—grief, guilt, fear, anger, and relief, all swirling together. In quiet moments, a deep sense of self-loathing engulfed me, heavy and suffocating. It intertwined with a profound despair that seemed to overshadow every flicker of hope. I feared for Landon's safety, his future, and whether I was capable of rising to meet the challenge.

Doubt crept in unexpectedly. Did I miss the signs? Am I to blame? Should I have spaced out his vaccines? Am I just a first-time mom trying to explain something that isn't even there?

But somewhere inside that chaos, something shifted. I made a choice: to follow my gut and learn. I buried myself in books, articles, forums—any space where people understood what this diagnosis meant. I found other parents walking similar paths. Slowly, the tide of fear began to recede, replaced by clarity. The more I learned, the more I began to see autism not as a limitation, but as a spectrum of extraordinary diversity.

With each connection I made, the path ahead became less frightening. I began to understand that Landon's differences weren't deficits. His intense focus and curiosity were incredible strengths. Instead of mourning what he wasn't, I started celebrating everything he was. His journey from who he was to who he is now beautifully illustrates the essence of an incredible human being.

Before Landon's diagnosis, my understanding of autism was limited and one-dimensional. I hadn't grasped how widely it could present—how every individual's experience could vary so greatly. I wrongly believed in a one-size-fits-all definition. That misunderstanding clouded my judgment and kept me from seeing the rich, nuanced beauty of who my son truly was.

As I grappled with my emotions and irrational thoughts, I felt like I was lost in a maze—confused, overwhelmed, and fearful of the future. I kept scrambling to "fix" him, searching for ways to help him fit into a world that had little patience for those who didn't conform. In my relentless pursuit of answers, I realized I was looking for solutions without truly understanding what needed addressing.

Over the following weeks, I made a conscious decision to slow down and simply observe. I noticed how he expressed his needs through gestures and sounds, how he showed kindness toward his toy trains, and how his curious mind worked to make sense of the world. Each day, I paid closer attention to his emotional cues, recognizing the gentleness and thoughtfulness behind them.

As my perspective shifted, I began to understand that my desire to "fix" him came from my fears—not from his limitations. I saw that I had been trying to solve a problem that didn't exist. Landon wasn't broken. He didn't need to be reassembled like a puzzle. He was already whole—brilliant and unique in his own right.

In truth, I realized that I had been both the problem and the solution. I had let a single diagnosis—a word on paper—overshadow the fullness of who he was. What Landon truly needed wasn't to be fixed; he needed someone to love, guide, support, teach, accept, and advocate for him in a world that often misunderstood him.

What he needed most was for me to understand his perspective. It wasn't about changing who he was but about meeting him where he stood. I learned that empathy and patience offered far more than any attempt to mold him into something more "typical." By opening my heart and mind, I could give him the unconditional love and support he deserved—allowing him to thrive on his own terms.

With renewed purpose, I stood by him as his mother and embraced the role of his advocate. I found therapies tailored to his needs and discovered an incredible school that celebrated diverse learning styles. Each small victory—every new word, every social interaction, every milestone—became a deeply cherished triumph.

As I stepped into this unexpected role, I began to redefine success—not by society's standards, but through moments that reflected Landon's perspective and growth.

Together, we navigated his journey one step at a time, forming a bond more resilient and profound than I had ever imagined.

Over time, I came to accept that the fear of parental failure would still resurface—but I was growing too. I was evolving alongside Landon. There was no manual to help me; my heart led the way. Love became our anchor, steadying us through uncertainty. And in the quiet moments, I could feel how deeply connected we had become. We were a team.

As I embraced this new chapter, I recognized that while the path ahead would be difficult, it was also full of opportunity and possibility. I was committed to walking beside him—celebrating his victories and supporting him through challenges. Each step forward, no matter how small, filled me with pride.

I found meaning in the joyful moments and uncovered lessons in the hard ones while teaching him to do the same. As our bond grew, I began to see the world through his eyes, gaining insight into the beauty of his unique view.

I learned to slow down and appreciate everything— the soothing sound of the rain hitting the window, embracing mistakes as opportunities for growth, sitting in silence with myself, and recognizing that skills require practice and patience to develop.

To support his progress, I created short-term and long-term goals tailored to his needs. Since he was too young to set them himself, I took on the responsibility. My priority was building a dedicated team of professionals who were committed to helping him grow.

Assembling the right team required research, time, and trust. In selecting each specialist, I prioritized not just their expertise, but their ability to listen and connect beyond what they learned in a textbook. I needed to know that we had a team who understood our journey and the choices we made along the way.

It wasn't easy—especially after being told for so long that everything was fine. That history made me cautious. But over time, I developed strong, trusting relationships with the doctors, therapists, and educators who joined our journey. That trust became the foundation of my son's developmental progress.

I emphasized open communication. We held regular check-ins, shared insights, and adjusted strategies together. This consistent, team-based approach offered Landon a sense of stability.

With every new goal reached, I saw his confidence grow. It was deeply rewarding to witness our shared efforts creating a nurturing environment where he could succeed and feel supported.

And somewhere in the midst of advocating for him, I found my own voice too. I had been so immersed in supporting Landon that I forgot about myself. I pushed through exhaustion, ignored the emotional strain, and wore a smile even when I felt like I was breaking inside.

Eventually, I realized that I couldn't pour from an empty cup. I needed space to breathe, to rest, and to reconnect with myself. Only then could I show up fully for my son—with clarity, presence, and determination.

Even though I had friends and family who made me laugh and offered distraction, I struggled to express the inner turmoil I was facing. The weight of my thoughts remained unspoken, locked beneath a polished exterior.

Joining an online support group and connecting with other parents who shared this path became a lifeline. When I finally began to open up about the challenges, something shifted. Expressing my feelings felt liberating. It was healing to be in a space where vulnerability was met with understanding.

My perspective began to evolve, and I learned not only to acknowledge my fears but also to recognize my strengths. I started tuning in to my own needs, learning that it was okay to ask for help, to admit exhaustion, and to voice my overwhelm. The parents in that group became more than just people—they became allies, cheerleaders, and an emotional safety net.

Through countless conversations, one truth became clear: to advocate for Landon, I first had to trust and believe in myself. I understood that strength wasn't about being unbreakable; it was about being self-aware, focused, and willing to learn and evolve. My vulnerabilities didn't weaken me—they fueled my resolve to fight for my son.

With each passing week, I found myself transforming. Armed with knowledge from shared experiences and professional insight, I approached school meetings and appointments with calm assertiveness. I no longer feared the unknown—I met it with clarity and confidence.

Eventually, I understood that this journey was as much about self-discovery as it was about advocacy. A space that once felt overwhelming began to feel like home. I was no longer just a worried, weary mother. I was becoming a confident advocate with the strength to stand in my truth. I learned to embrace differences, continued learning about everything and anything, and responded—when needed—to those who questioned our experience with judgment or ignorance.

After Landon's diagnosis, many people seemed to have something to say about autism. Outsiders who had never walked our path felt compelled to offer unsolicited opinions and ignorant comments. Some approached gently and with compassion, while others arrived with outdated beliefs or assumptions. Regardless of their intent, many shared two things in common: they thought they understood, and I'd allow the disrespect.

I often found myself being flooded with questions, comments, and unsolicited advice, usually introduced with phrases like:

"Have you considered...?"

"You should try..."

"Someone needs a nap..."

"Can he really...?"

"Why does he...?"

"He'll never…"

"Oh, he's fine."

"That's weird, I've never seen that before…"

"He's nine—he can do it."

"He'll grow out of it."

"Stop babying him."

"What's wrong with him?"

My responses varied depending on who was speaking, their tone, and whether they had a relationship with Landon or me. In hindsight, I know I sometimes reacted too harshly—especially toward those who meant well but lacked awareness. For that, I offer a sincere apology. I now realize they, too, were speaking from a place of limited knowledge—a place I once stood in myself.

I've come to believe that kindness can exist even in missteps. While I regret the intensity of some of my reactions, I do not apologize to those who ignored my boundaries or stood on the other side of my exhaustion. Some lessons are best taught by silence, others through dialogue. I believe that through empathy, patience, and shared understanding, we can build a more compassionate conversation about autism—one rooted in listening understanding, and perspective, not assumptions.

Writing this book has brought everything into focus. As I reviewed old journals, session notes from early intervention, private therapy records, and school records, I was flooded with emotion. Each journal entry reminded me of Landon's extraordinary journey, even the early years marked by steep challenges—moments that often felt insurmountable.

As I laid out everything I had about his journey across my living room floor to write this book, I reflected on the small victories, breakthroughs, and tools that helped him find his way. The therapists, teachers, case managers, doctors, bus drivers, athletic coaches, and aides all played significant roles in shaping his experience and transforming struggle into progress, one moment at a time. I am incredibly grateful to each of them.

 I remember how hard it once was for Landon to communicate his needs, enjoy a movie, blow bubbles, succeed at hopscotch, ride a bike, tie his shoes, use the toilet, follow instructions, hold a pencil, and connect with other children.

Those moments were difficult for both of us—filled with uncertainty and quiet fears about the future.

From the moment he took his first breath, every memory has become a reminder of his incredible strength and resilience. Watching him embrace strategies that once felt unfamiliar—now part of his daily rhythm—is nothing short of remarkable. I couldn't be more proud of him.

I'm equally grateful for the steady love and support of our close friends and family who have stood by us through every challenge. Having them made me realize that everyone needs support at some point—whether in personal life, school, or work. Through Landon's journey, I've been profoundly changed. He has not only shaped who I am as a person, but even more so as a mother.

At just 18 years old, he's already achieved so much. He excels personally, academically and athletically, volunteers in his community, and pursues his passions with genuine enthusiasm. He works hard every day to face his fears and improve his social interaction. His determination to make a difference through his chosen field—Culinary—is nothing short of inspiring. His dreams are within reach because he maintains focus and works hard to make those dreams—a reality.

He meets difficulties head-on and continues to rise with strength and purpose. Watching him grow has enriched my life in countless ways and reminded me daily of the lessons we hold close: love, perseverance, empathy, patience, compassion, and the power of ambition. I have no doubt that Landon will keep thriving. His story is still unfolding, and it's clear he's on a path filled with promise.

CHAPTER *10*

You Can Help More Than You Know

As we worked through the complexities of testing, doctor appointments, therapy sessions, school adjustments, and the countless challenges of daily life, I found myself constantly searching for meaningful ways to support and nurture Landon. One of the most important lessons I've learned as a mother is this: before focusing on the specifics of autism—or any—diagnosis start by understanding your child as an individual.

By observing their behavior, listening closely to their thoughts, empathizing with their feelings, and recognizing the unique traits that define them, you will gain clarity on how to connect with them. Every child with autism experiences the world in their own way, so it's essential to discover how it shapes your child's communication, learning, and interactions. This awareness helps reveal their strengths, highlights areas where support may be needed, and uncovers personal preferences that are sometimes overlooked.

This kind of understanding deepened my relationship with my son. It allowed me to connect more intentionally with his passions, dreams, and hobbies. I came to see how much he loves languages, numbers, sharks, horror films, WWE, "Would You Rather" questions, bowling, art, food—and how remarkably talented he is at building intricate models. These interests opened the door to countless engaging activities and became springboards for his creativity and growth.

Because every person with autism is unique, it was critical that I treat Landon's experience as his own—not as part of a single, uniform condition. After his diagnosis, I understood that every decision going forward would have lasting effects on his development. At times, I overanalyzed, second-guessed myself, and rushed into services that later proved ineffective. There were no shortcuts—only time, trials, and patience. Together, we had to learn what worked and what didn't.

Transitions and Schedule Changes

Transitions—from one activity or place to another—often left Landon feeling overwhelmed and anxious. Even small shifts in his routine could feel like sudden storms. Navigating those changes became one of our daily challenges.

After his diagnosis, everything began to shift. His doctors and therapists emphasized the need for routine and structure to help him feel secure. I remember sitting at our kitchen table, surrounded by colorful markers and large sheets of paper, carefully creating a daily schedule. That schedule became a lifeline.

Every part of the day was planned, from breakfast to bedtime. The consistency helped Landon feel more grounded. To make things even clearer, I introduced visual schedules—words and images that represented each activity. A picture of a sunny park for playtime. A cozy book for Storytime. A plate of food on the table for mealtimes. These visuals became his guideposts, reducing anxiety and offering a sense of predictability.

Landon thrived within that structure. Our mornings were filled with comforting rituals: the smell of waffles and eggs, the familiar sound of cartoons playing softly in the background, and his trains arranged just how he liked them. That predictability gave him a sense of safety—a calm, familiar rhythm he could rely on.

As the days passed, I made it a habit to talk to him about the day ahead. We'd sit together, looking at the colorful schedule, and I'd say things like, *"After lunch, we'll visit the library,"* pointing to the picture of an open book. *"Let's pack some snacks, juice, and water too."*

Consistency and repetition became our ally. Using the same phrases, providing step by step instructions with demonstrations, and encouraging Landon to repeat the plan back to me, helped him internalize the routine. Each time he practiced a new transition—like completing his homework after school before play—he grew more confident. Little by little, transitions became less daunting.

Life, however, had its own plans, often throwing unexpected curveballs that disrupted our carefully built routine. One cool October morning, a hurricane swept through town causing schools to close for weeks. Landon's sense of stability unraveled in a matter of days. Instead of learning and playing with friends, he was faced with frustration and confusion. His safe spaces felt compromised, and the resulting meltdown echoed through the house. It became painfully clear: while routines provided structure, they couldn't always protect Landon from life's unpredictability.

After months of navigating these turbulent moments, I realized the need for something more—balance. I knew I couldn't control every storm, but I believed I could teach Landon how to manage the unexpected. Slowly, I began introducing flexibility into our routines, helping him build resilience when life didn't go according to plan.

In the quiet of our evenings, I would sit on the couch and draft daily schedules, this time including the possibility of change. *"Some things might change today,"* I'd explain, gently preparing him. We started having conversations about disappointment and problem-solving. If a plan was canceled, I'd hold him close and say*, "We'll try again another day,"* or *"It's okay—now we can go to the park instead."*

Over time, something incredible began to happen. The little boy who once struggled with even the smallest changes started to adapt. One rainy afternoon, Landon looked outside and calmly said, *"No outside. Morrow, Mommy!"* —a simple sentence, yet a monumental victory. There was no frustration, no meltdown—just understanding and acceptance.

His ability to manage changes grew stronger with time. When unexpected events popped up, he adjusted. He'd make a plan to do or catch up on homework, rearrange his schedule if things came up unexpectedly, and even suggest alternatives for missed activities. The structure we'd built had become a trampoline—something he could bounce back from, not a rigid frame that confined him.

His fear of unpredictability gave way to curiosity, decision-making, and problem-solving. He began expressing his feelings clearly, discussing possible solutions, and approaching challenges with a maturity that impressed everyone around him. The boy who once resisted change had evolved into a young man who welcomed it.

Through these struggles and triumphs, Landon developed strong organizational and time-management skills—ones that reached far beyond the classroom. He became more self-reliant, managing his responsibilities with growing independence. And with that came something even more powerful: confidence.

Reflecting on his growth, I've come to understand how essential that balance truly was. Routine gave Landon security, but flexibility gave him freedom. He wasn't just following a schedule anymore—he was learning how to navigate life.

Taking a Step Back

Landon's path required both of us to grow in ways we hadn't anticipated following his diagnosis. I poured myself into supporting him—planning every detail, adjusting routines, and tracking every milestone. Each morning and evening, I would sit with my notebook, reviewing the day's successes and preparing goals for the next. Even when he couldn't fully understand, I would tell him how proud I was. *"You did a great job today,"* I'd say, making sure he felt seen and acknowledged, even in silence.

Communication became a foundation of our journey. Through consistency, repetition, gentle reminders, patience, and redirection, I guided him through unfamiliar situations. Each small achievement became a celebration. I can still see the way his face lit up when I cheered him on. *"You did it! I'm so proud of you!"* I'd exclaim—not just to encourage him, but to build the belief that he could do hard things.

But as days turned into weeks, and weeks into months, something shifted. I began to realize—through both observation and quiet reflection—that I didn't need to intervene all the time. Landon was learning to lead. Equipped with tools, strategies, and a growing inner strength, he stepped forward on his own.

At first, the idea of stepping back felt daunting. I had grown so accustomed to holding his hand through every challenge that letting go—even slightly—felt unnatural. *"You've got this, my prince,"* I whispered in my mind, even as my instincts pulled me to intervene. But over time, I learned to trust Landon's direction. He began to speak up when he felt ready to take on tasks alone. *"Mom, I think I can do this one myself,"* he'd say, with a quiet confidence that made my heart swell—even as a trace of worry lingered.

Moments like those were turning points for me. I realized that allowing Landon to explore his independence didn't lessen the importance of my support—it just reshaped it. I began to embrace this new balance. I watched him take ownership of projects, sketch out blueprints, and build prototypes, each one a symbol of his growing autonomy. He was becoming the young man I had always believed he could be.

Ultimately, I came to understand that being a loving, supportive mother wasn't about controlling every step—it was about laying the foundation for him to stand tall, guiding him gently as he uncovered his strength.

Letting go was transformative. Rather than feeling like I was losing him, I saw it as a new chapter in motherhood—one where I could stand back and admire the young person emerging. It gave me space to reflect on the beautiful moments we'd shared: his first steps, late-night talks about his dreams and fears, and the countless times he turned to me for guidance. I cherished those memories and how they shaped the remarkable young man now standing before me.

Strengths Conquer Weakness

With a heart full of passion and a mind brimming with imagination, Landon found solace in the world of trains. Thomas the Tank Engine was his favorite, and he adored the bright colors, whimsical characters, and adventurous tales that unfolded on the tracks. Whenever he felt overwhelmed, he would turn to Thomas for joy, calling for his dad or me to join in. We'd gather around, laughing and playing together in a world where everything made sense to him.

As he grew, his interests began to blossom—like spring flowers stretching toward the sun. One day, while

flipping through channels, his dad stumbled upon a WWE match. Landon's eyes lit up with fascination. The wrestlers moved with power and theatrical flair, capturing his imagination instantly. These athletes became larger-than-life heroes in his mind, and soon he was cheering from the couch, mimicking the crowd's excitement.

That moment sparked a new passion. Thomas began to fade into the background as wrestling took center stage.

Landon started reenacting the matches around the house, transforming his toys into contenders and his floor into a makeshift wrestling ring. He'd challenge his friends and family, his creativity fueling every bout.

I can still hear the laughter that filled the room the day he challenged his godfather in the living room. His godfather graciously played the underdog, drawing cheers from all of us as Landon claimed the title. *"Heavyweight Champion!"* we all shouted in unison, celebrating his victory with joy that echoed through the walls.

His bedroom soon transformed into a WWE sanctuary—posters lined the walls, action figures filled his shelves, and his passion radiated from every corner. It was more than just a phase—it was a world where Landon felt strong, confident, and fully himself.

Wrestling wasn't just a pastime for Landon—it became a catalyst for growth. Through his passion, he began to improve his communication skills, often narrating the action like a ringside commentator. As he played with friends, he practiced teamwork, learning to collaborate and show respect—even in the heat of playful competition. Wrestling also became an outlet for his creativity, allowing him to express feelings and build elaborate storylines and characters that brought his imagination to life.

One evening, during a particularly intense match, Landon turned to me with wide eyes and said, *"One day, I want to go to WrestleMania!"* I smiled, knowing just how much that dream meant to him. He still talks about it often—the day he'll sit in the audience, cheering for his heroes and hoping to meet them in person. Someday, I hope to turn that dream into reality.

Challenges will always arise, but sometimes it's the passions we hold most dearly that reveal the strengths we never knew we had. I witnessed that transformation firsthand. What began as a fascination with trains evolved into a love for the bold, theatrical world of WWE. This wasn't just a change in hobbies—it marked the beginning of something bigger.

Landon started setting goals for himself after observing how hard wrestlers worked to earn title belts, gain fans, and build strength. He approached each goal with focus and determination, imagining what he could achieve by putting in that same level of effort. As he accomplished his goals and witnessed the results, his confidence grew—along with his skills. These small victories broadened his horizons, introducing him to new experiences and perspectives that he may never have encountered otherwise.

Through every passion and interest, he encountered, Landon transformed challenges into strengths. What once felt like hurdles became stepping stones. He embraced his capabilities and began using them to navigate life's twists with greater resilience. Today, he stands grounded and self-assured, carrying the courage, joy, and determination his passions helped uncover—ready to face whatever lies ahead.

Downtime

Many days, Landon and I felt completely drained like we were adrift in uncharted waters. Each day brought a relentless wave of appointments: early intervention evaluations, doctor visits, endless blood draws, and therapy sessions that seemed to stretch endlessly. The constant need to adapt—to new strategies, new behaviors, new situations, new schedules, and new expectations—was emotionally exhausting. I longed to reclaim a sense of autonomy, to carve out moments that felt truly ours. But I often had no idea where to begin.

Whenever activities were canceled or the weather disrupted our plans, we embraced cozy days at home, especially after I managed to calm his meltdown. These moments became pockets of tranquility in our otherwise hectic routine. We would work on various skills together—

speech, sensory play, reading, mealtimes, tying shoes, buttoning and zipping coats, potty training, and even simple chores. However, not every day went smoothly.

One afternoon, Landon was especially uncooperative. Instead of pushing forward, I decided to pause. I allowed him to express whatever he needed— without pressure and expectations. I put him in his safari jumper and watched as he bounced with wild abandon. Sometimes, his movements were soft and rhythmic; other times, they shook the room. He loved that jumper and could enjoy it a little longer since he was so little. It gave him the sensory stimulation his body craved and a safe space to release his energy. Eventually, his bouncing slowed, and he drifted off to sleep soon after.

I felt relieved as I unbuckled him gently and carried him to his crib, settling him under the mobile's soft lullabies. Then, I made my way to the couch, sinking into its plush cushions and took a deep breath. This was the "me time" I had longed for.

I reached for the remote, my fingers trembling slightly as I turned on Lifetime, letting its familiar dramas take me somewhere far from the noise of the day. The silence felt like a warm blanket—soothing, unfamiliar, and deeply needed. In that stillness, I realized how vital these breaks were. We needed them—to breathe, to regroup, and simply to be.

During our hardest weeks, I made a conscious decision to disconnect from anything that added stress. We unplugged from the world outside and turned inward. There were no appointments and no structured plans—just space, time, and stillness. And it made all the difference.

We napped, played, and let the day unfold without deadlines. Landon thrived during those moments, fully immersed in his natural rhythms. He stimmed freely—those repetitive, self-soothing movements bringing him comfort and peace. It was beautiful to witness. He wasn't just passing time; he was restoring himself.

As I watched him, I felt a deep, quiet gratitude. I saw how vital it was for him to explore his environment on his own terms, to create his own sense of safety and control. In those moments, my little birdie was free—navigating his world with pure joy, unburdened by external demands.

In my relentless search for solutions, I had once overlooked something essential: the power of rest. I thought progress meant constant doing. But I've come to understand that reflection, stillness, and space are not pauses in the journey—they're part of the journey. Now, I embrace that truth wholeheartedly. And I hold no regrets.

Meltdowns

One afternoon, Landon sat at his little Thomas the Train table, surrounded by a circle of engines. His hands moved quickly, pushing the trains across the track, his wide eyes locked in concentration. He was completely immersed, narrating an imaginary journey with expressive sound effects and dialogue. As he raced toward a destination only he could see, I accidentally bumped the edge of the table. The trains jolted, derailing the world he had so carefully constructed.

He turned to me, his expression full of disbelief—How could you? In an instant, frustration crashed over him like a wave. The trains tumbled to the floor, followed by tears and a full-body meltdown. He dropped to the ground, consumed by the sudden loss of control.

As the emotional storm intensified, I knew the most important thing I could do was simply stay close and steady. I didn't try to stop the tears. I didn't rush to fix the scene. Instead, I stayed present—offering calm, silent support while his feelings ran their course. Every emotion was valid, even when they arrived in overwhelming bursts.

Eventually, the sobs softened. The storm quieted to a drizzle. When the timing felt right, I gently guided him to the couch, away from the scattered trains and the scene of disruption. I settled him into my lap, aligning our eyes and wrapping my arms around him. I wanted him to feel seen, safe, and grounded—like he was landing back in familiar territory.

"What were you feeling when I accidentally bumped your train table?" I asked softly, using a voice I hoped would create a space for trust. Landon stared at the floor, his small fingers twisting the hem of his shirt, his mouth pressed to its edge.

The effort to find the right words showed on his face, so, I offered a gentle nudge. *"It's completely okay to feel frustrated. Everyone feels that way sometimes."* I paused, then added, *"And I'm really sorry I bumped into your table."*

His bottom lip quivered. He nodded slowly, eyes rising to meet mine. I could see relief in his gaze—relief that his feelings were seen, even if he still struggled to name them. Together, we explored possible solutions. *"What if we line the trains back up together?"* I suggested. *"And maybe we can find a spot where your table won't get bumped again?"* Bit by bit, his frown faded. Small nods turned into smiles as he returned to the joyful world he had just experienced moments ago.

In the days and weeks that followed, I began to understand the patterns behind Landon's meltdowns better.

A sudden honk from a passing car, music playing too loud, a flash of lightning during a storm, or an itchy tag on a shirt could all disrupt his calm. His reactions weren't random—they were signals.

So, I adjusted. I dimmed the living room lights to soften the space. I lowered the volume of our playlist, closed the curtains during a storm, and swapped scratchy clothes for soft fabrics that wouldn't irritate his skin or distract him.

Even snacks became part of our emotional toolkit. On quieter days, a handful of animal crackers gave him something predictable and satisfying to enjoy. On high-stress days, the crunch of a chocolate chip cookie seemed to melt tension away, offering comfort in the most ordinary but meaningful way.

I closely observed how he interacted with his peers. Play often brought joy, but at times it sparked confusion or conflict, leaving him feeling apart from the group. Through watching these moments unfold, I learned how to support him by encouraging connections while honoring his need for space.

Over time, Landon began recognizing and naming his emotions in his own way. *"Too loud or Stop,"* he'd say when loud music or noises overwhelmed him, or *"sticky"* and *"yuck"* when a new food felt wrong. His meltdowns gradually decreased as I began to anticipate and meet his needs more effectively.

The once-frequent outbursts gave way to emerging coping strategies. One afternoon, his face lit up as he recounted feeling overwhelmed earlier in the day. *"Big breath,"* he said proudly, *"and then I count to ten!"*

In that moment, joy washed over me. I realized that giving Landon space to feel—and helping him understand those feelings—was guiding him toward self-regulation.

Downtime allowed him to be himself and pursue his interests. It gave me the opportunity to observe how he managed without any guidance. During the quiet moments, as I reflected on his struggles and achievements, I felt deeply grateful for the laughter, tears, and steady growth that transformed our home into a haven of hope.

Sensory

Landon has long experienced challenges tied to sensory processing, particularly involving touch, movement, balance, and body awareness. His strong aversion to certain textures influences everyday decisions—what he eats, what he wears, and even how he engages with art and other activities. Some fabrics feel itchy or restrictive against his skin, leading him to avoid clothing others might find comfortable. Sounds like fire alarms, screeching doors, or vacuum cleaners—background noise to most—became unbearable, often triggering distress or anxiety.

Physical activities like stair climbing were difficult, yet he delighted in movement-based experiences like jumping and spinning. These kinetic activities matched his sensory preferences and offered comfort and joy. Basic tasks—tying shoelaces, zipping coats, turning doorknobs, putting on his shoes—challenged his motor skills. He often sat in a W position on the floor, a posture that seemed to calm and stabilize him when things felt overwhelming.

His sensitivity to clothing has been a constant thread throughout his life. Certain garments feel like they're scratching or pinching, a discomfort that's hard to describe but visibly frustrating for him. When he was younger, this often led to awkward walking, visible anxiety, meltdowns, or even social withdrawal.

As he's grown, Landon has shown more flexibility in his preferences. He's become more open to trying new foods—particularly vegan and plant-based dishes—though he still clings to familiar favorites. Interestingly, he continues to wear his socks inside out unless we find a pair that meets his comfort standards. He prefers athletic clothing, especially polyester, and insists on trying on garments during shopping trips to ensure they meet his sensory needs.

Brands like Adidas, Champion, Nike, and Under Armour remain Landon's top picks, thanks to their soft and breathable fabrics. Denim, however, has never been comfortable for him—he's only worn it a handful of times and not without a complete meltdown. I've searched for jeans with gentler linings and insulation, hoping to ease the discomfort, but the waistband and heaviness continues to pose a challenge.

Finding suitable formal wear remains difficult, as most stores don't account for tactile sensitivity, making each outing feel like a mission. There have been countless times we've struggled to find clothes that meet Landon's needs.

Still, he often gathers himself with quiet determination, especially when choices are limited. Even in moments of discomfort, he reminds himself that he can get through it. To provide him with ease and additional comfort, we often bring extra clothing in case he has the opportunity to change.

One moment that stands out took place at my best friend's wedding in August 2024, where Landon proudly served as ring security. He understood that being part of the celebration meant wearing the formal outfit selected for him. My best friend expressed genuine pride in his willingness to stretch beyond his comfort zone for their big day. In a thoughtful gesture, she assured him he could change into something more comfortable right after the photos. That understanding made all the difference.

The transformation was instant. As soon as he changed, his shoulders relaxed, a wide smile appeared, and it was clear he was ready to enjoy the rest of the evening. Watching him light up on the dance floor—carefree, confident, and joyful—was unforgettable. I later shared with my best friend how much that moment meant to me. Her expression said it all—she understood his effort came from love, and in return, hers did too.

When Landon doesn't feel well, describing what he's experiencing can be tricky. If he has a headache, he might say his head hurts but struggle to explain how. Sharp or throbbing? He doesn't always know. He uses the word "headache" as a catch-all, and if someone compares it to something like being kicked, he can't relate if he hasn't had that experience and can't measure his pain on a scale others might find useful.

Pain scales, in general, feel meaningless to him. He sees pain as one sensation—bad—and resists assigning it a number. Rather than describe it, he focuses on making it stop. His low pain tolerance means he works hard to avoid pain altogether—opting out of certain activities, seeking help early, or leaning on coping tools. For him, relief matters more than categorizing.

Loud sounds caused him anxiety and made him fear everything around him. Headphones became his savior, helping him block out both familiar and unexpected noises. Through various trials, Landon adapted and developed coping strategies that allowed him to face auditory challenges with greater confidence.

He enjoys loud music, often cranking up the volume to immerse himself in the vibrant beats. However, he is mindful of his surroundings and knows when to lower the sound for a moment of tranquility. He no longer relies on headphones and has found comfort in knowing he can cover his ears with his hands or seek help from others if things become too loud.

One of my favorite things is turning up the volume in the car and watching him come alive to his favorite songs. As the music fills the space, his whole body moves—swaying, nodding, lip syncing every word he knows by heart. His joy is so complete, so present, that it brings tears to my eyes. In those moments, surrounded by our shared playlist, I'm overwhelmed with gratitude—for every person who's walked beside him, supported him, encouraged him, and helped shape these beautiful, ordinary moments into something extraordinary.

Building Confidence Through Sports, Hobbies, Ambitions, and Other Interests

Bowling

Sports combine fun, competition, and achievement, creating memorable moments. My family has a long-standing tradition in baseball and softball, so I assumed Landon might follow that same path. He tried a range of sports but quickly realized that many didn't suit his strengths due to sensory sensitivities, coordination challenges, and slower processing speed and reaction times.

Eventually, he discovered that individual sports like track, swimming, bowling, and martial arts gave him more freedom and control. We agreed to focus on the ones that matched his needs—and Landon thrived. He chose to dedicate himself to bowling, where he found both joy and success.

Landon's love for bowling began when he was five. In high school, he tried out and made the varsity team—a milestone that brought him great pride. At first, he bowled straight, but he was eager to learn how to hook the ball and understand lane conditions. With support from a skilled coach, he mastered the hook, building confidence and consistency. By the end of his freshman year, he had bowled a 172 high game and a 489 series, which motivated him to join leagues, compete in tournaments, and work with various skilled coaches.

By sophomore year, Landon had become a focused bowler—competing more with himself than with others. He celebrated others' victories, always showing strong sportsmanship. That year, he bowled his first 200-game with a 205, then topped it with a 232 high game and a 531 series.

Each bowling season brings renewed excitement. In junior year, Landon proudly served as varsity team captain, recognized for his strong qualities, ability and leadership. His teammates—and even his competitors—respected him. He ended the year with a 162 average, a 216 high game, and a 580 series. After every season, he sets new goals, a habit I truly admire.

Senior year was filled with emotion and determination. One memory that stands out is his first and last bowl of the season—something I'll always hold dear. He achieved a personal best 611 series and a record-setting 241

high game. The magnitude of his performance didn't hit him right away, but the pride in his eyes said it all. His team advanced to the state championships, where he bowled with remarkable consistency, averaging 220. He wrapped up his high school career with a 175 average, a four-year varsity plaque, MVP honors, a scholarship, and All-County and All-Conference Honorable Mentions.

Throughout his journey, Landon has earned a strong support system—both in person and online. Many family members and friends have come to watch him play, and the joy it brings him is breathtaking. He bowled his first-ever 600 series at the

Special Olympics, taking first place. However, the moment was made even more special by having his extended family, whom he adores, there to witness and cheer him on.

His perseverance in the Special Olympics has earned him 1st and 2nd place finishes at district, sectional, and state levels. Participation in leagues and tournaments has led to scholarship awards, recognizing both his talent and dedication. He's collected an impressive array of trophies and awards: Athlete of the Season, Most Dedicated Player, MVP, and more—all symbols of his hard work and determination.

Along the way, Landon has bowled alongside some of the best. He's trained with skilled mentors and even met professionals like Bill O'Neill, EJ Tackett, Jason Belmonte, and Kyle Troup at his first PBA tournament in 2024—a dream come true. Getting his first bowling ball signed by them was a moment he'll never forget.

I never imagined my son would be a bowler, but I'm endlessly proud that he found something he truly loves. His dedication, his willingness to learn, and his ability to push through challenges have shaped him into a remarkable athlete. Whether he's seeking advice, practicing techniques, challenging himself, or facing pressure, he stays grounded, determined, and optimistic.

The bowling community has embraced Landon with kindness and support. Coaches, teammates, and parents create an environment where growth and friendship flourish. Watching him rise to each challenge whether it's a strike, a spare, or a frustrating split—reminds me that commitment and encouragement are what truly matter.

Art

From an early age, Landon showed a deep love for art. While he wasn't drawn to messy projects, he gravitated toward precision—coloring in and out of the lines, tracing with care, and expressing his creativity through control. As he got older, his passion grew. He explored websites, YouTube tutorials, and art books, immersing himself in new ideas and techniques.

Drawing became both a relaxing escape and a source of excitement. Often, before finishing one piece, his mind would already be racing with the next idea. He keeps an art journal filled with his creations, documenting his evolution as an artist and celebrating his unique vision.

Landon draws daily, refining his technique through consistent practice. Tracing exercises have also helped him strengthen his fine motor skills. He participates in online art classes and eagerly explores new methods, always hungry for inspiration.

Art has not only sharpened Landon's technical skills but also boosted his confidence. Knowing he can create pieces that others find difficult empowers him. Art has become a core part of who he is, and he dreams of continuing this path in the future.

Landon's creative energy extends to the kitchen, too. His goal of becoming a chef fits beautifully with his artistic nature. He enjoys imagining inventive dishes, blending flavors, and presenting meals with the same care and vision he brings to his drawings.

Culinary

During his junior year, Landon took a bold step and enrolled in Vocational school to pursue his love of cooking. He embraced the challenge of splitting his days between Votech in the mornings and high school in the afternoons. Now a senior, he thrives in this balanced routine—focusing on academics in the morning and refining his culinary skills each afternoon.

At first, Landon's food allergies limited what he could taste, which was understandably frustrating. But his teacher—affectionately called "Chef"—made thoughtful adjustments, using dairy-free, rice-free, and barley-free ingredients so Landon could enjoy the meals. Seeing him included in these shared moments was truly heartwarming.

Through the program, he's learned to handle a variety of knives with precision and confidence— chopping, dicing, peeling—and has become skilled in techniques such as sautéing, frying, and baking. He's also teamed up with classmates to prepare meals for events and holiday celebrations.

Landon has proudly served as Sous Chef and taken the lead at various stations throughout the program. Alongside building strong friendships, one of the most touching experiences has been his choice to learn sign language to better communicate with classmates who are deaf or hard of hearing. Although an interpreter is present in the kitchen, Landon explained that these students are his friends, and he wanted to connect with them directly. This decision speaks volumes about his empathy and character.

To support this goal, I enrolled him in a sign language class—an experience that has expanded his communication skills and deepened his commitment to inclusivity in the culinary world.

Landon's passion for cooking also includes a strong focus on food safety, hygiene, and maintaining a clean and efficient kitchen. He's dedicated to learning about allergies, sanitation, storage, equipment, and fire safety—because for him, cooking is not just about the food. It's about creating a welcoming, safe space where everyone feels valued.

Other Interests

Landon has a wide range of interests that bring him both comfort and confidence. One of his standout strengths is his incredible attention to detail. He can spend hours deeply focused on a single task, whether he's building intricate Lego sets or solving challenging puzzles.

These activities weren't always easy. In the past, he struggled with frustration and self-doubt. But driven by his love for these pastimes, he refused to give up.

Landon also enjoys watching food challenge videos on YouTube—especially those featuring outrageous eating feats. He also gets a kick out of scary and silly pranks that make him laugh or jump. He regularly watches bowling highlights and drills to sharpen his game and stays engaged with interactive trivia and games that test his knowledge while keeping things fun.

In his downtime, Landon loves playing cards and word games. Rummy 500 and Blackjack let him think strategically, while Sudoku pushes him to apply logic in new ways. He also enjoys word searches, word scrambles, hidden pictures, and sticker-by-number projects, which combine mental engagement with relaxation and creativity.

One of his favorite games is "Would You Rather?"—a conversation starter that sparks laughter and thoughtful discussion with friends and family. He also loves board games, with Monopoly ranking high on his list for its blend of competition and strategy.

That said, losing doesn't always come easy for Landon. When he faces defeat, it can take a toll on his mood. To help him manage those feelings, I remind him that losing is part of life—and not a reflection of his worth. I encourage him to see each loss as a learning opportunity, not a failure. I teach him that all losses can become wins if he embraces the lessons learned from them.

CHAPTER *11*

───❧───

The Beauty of His World

When autism entered our lives, I was overwhelmed by fear—afraid I might never truly connect with my son the way I saw other parents connect with their children. That fear was shaped by the portrayals I'd seen in movies and the misconceptions I had unknowingly absorbed. But over time, I realized that our experience has been more rewarding than I ever anticipated. I made a conscious choice to embrace Landon exactly as he is, to see beyond the label and celebrate the person in front of me—his personality, his affection, his strengths, his spark.

Sharing in Landon's hobbies has opened a door into his world. Each activity reveals something new—another piece of who he is—and deepens my love and appreciation for him. Watching his courage as he lives authentically, without trying to conform to others' expectations, inspires me daily.

I've come to understand that the fear of judgment can silence people from expressing their true selves. But Landon, despite facing rejection, bullying, and misunderstanding, remains steadfastly himself. His ability to stay true under pressure is one of his greatest strengths. It reminds me, every day, that authenticity isn't just brave—it's powerful. In many ways, autism has given him—and all of us—a reason to recognize and celebrate that truth.

Because of Landon, I push myself to be better. Our journey together has shown me that resilience, patience, compassion, and honesty can shape a bond built on mutual understanding and love.

What amazes me is how he turns his interests into strengths—how he uses them to engage with the world and accept his imperfections. His love for what he does shields him from outside judgment, helping him build a quiet resilience I deeply admire. Each obstacle he faces seems to feed his determination and watching that determination has inspired growth in me as well.

Landon has developed a strong curiosity about human behavior—primarily actions that hurt others, like lying or being unkind. He notices these behaviors around him and doesn't hesitate to speak up. I always validate his feelings, letting him know it's perfectly okay to feel confused or upset by such actions. While others' behavior is beyond our control, I explain our choices are not. I encourage him to think about the experiences that might lead someone to act that way, even when we can't fully understand them. I always remind him of his kind nature, and how compassionately responding to unkindness is his quiet strength.

This mindset has shaped how he continues to treat others. When someone speaks negatively about themselves, Landon responds with kindness. He points out what makes them special, helping them see their worth. He chooses silence when others speak with cruelty—not always out of fear, but because he knows that adding to the negativity solves nothing. In those moments, I see his deep sense of empathy in action.

But it's also painful to admit that others don't always show him the same kindness he offers. When that happens, I remind him of his values and worth. I teach him that it's okay to step away from people who try to diminish him. We talk about how those behaviors often say more about the other person than about him. Through these conversations, he's learning that he has the right to choose relationships that make him feel respected and safe.

In our talks, I often reflect on the idea of "normal" — what it means, and whether it's even something to strive for. I remind Landon that differences are something to celebrate, not hide. Normal doesn't exist because we'd all be the same if it did. Our differences are part of what makes each person unique.

I'm especially proud of how he views his autism—not as something that holds him back, but as something that shapes his perspective in meaningful ways. He knows that being autistic doesn't lessen his worth—it deepens his identity. Watching him take pride in that is deeply moving.

As he becomes more comfortable with who he is, I see him step into social situations with quiet confidence. He's learning that being different isn't a weakness—it's a strength. That realization gives him the courage to try new things, approach new situations, explore different avenues, and build genuine connections while staying grounded in himself.

Landon's emotions are shaped by his daily experiences. As his mother, I get to witness the full spectrum—his bursts of joy when something excites him, his moments of frustration when things don't go as planned. I can't read his mind—though some days it feels like I can—but I've developed a strong sense for when something is off. When I notice a shift, I gently ask him how he's feeling or what's on his mind, giving him space to open up. At times there is nothing at all, while at other times, he will ask, *"How do you know when something is bothering me?" "I just pay attention, that's all,"* I say with a laugh.

There are times when my questions don't receive immediate answers. Landon processes information at his own pace. He needs time to absorb what I've said, reflect on it, and respond thoughtfully. Sometimes, he requires me to express it differently. These pauses, although they may feel long, are often essential for him.

Landon has a sincere and unwavering desire for meaningful connection. He longs for spaces where he feels truly seen, understood, accepted, and safe—where he can be himself without fear. I often find myself wondering why it is so difficult for some people to embrace who he is, especially when he offers that acceptance so readily. But then I remind myself that he is not like everyone else, and it's clear that not everyone possesses his admirable character.

His world—the one I have the privilege of being a part of—opened my eyes to truths I had once avoided. And now, I hold tightly to the promise that he will see not the harshness of this world, but the beauty within it. While society can be unkind, his world is one of vibrant color, laughter, and light. It is my mission to protect that space— to nurture an environment where his innocence can thrive, untouched by cruelty and full of warmth and joy.

Patience is something I didn't fully understand until I became his mother. It changed everything. I practiced it daily—until it became second nature—because he needed me to show up for him, just as much as I needed to understand him. Patience helped me slow down, pause, breathe, gather my thoughts, and find strength in the unknown. Patience taught me to take it one day a time. Though autism is a formal diagnosis, I've come to see it as a different way of experiencing the world—one that calls for empathy, openness, and compassion.

But the lessons Landon has taught me go far beyond patience. He has shown me strength when I felt weak, reminding me that resilience often shows itself in the toughest moments. He gave me hope when I felt lost. He brought clarity when I couldn't see a way forward. And just when I felt empty, he offered love so pure and powerful that it pulled me back from despair. He kept me moving when uncertainty made me want to give up.

In him, I found purpose again. Through his presence, I learned to see beauty in the midst of hardship—to hold on to connection when I thought I had nothing left.

CHAPTER *12*

What I Never Knew... I Know Now

While I always believed that having a child would be a blessing, I've come to understand that the fears and challenges that accompany motherhood are equally valuable. They've shaped me in ways I never expected. Motherhood has revealed a reality marked by constant sacrifice, abandoned plans, sleepless nights, and emotions I couldn't have imagined before my son was born.

When I first learned I was pregnant, I thought little about the what-ifs—who really does? I was so overjoyed by the idea of becoming a mother that I didn't focus on what could go wrong.

But as the days turned into sleepless nights, it quickly became clear that the image I had carried—the dreamy, romantic version of motherhood—was only a small part of the truth. My love for my son is immeasurable, yet it often walks hand in hand with doubt, fatigue, and worry.

Navigating this new world has been both beautiful and overwhelming. I've spent countless hours learning to adapt, trying to find balance while staying in tune with his needs.

In the midst of it all, I discovered the quiet beauty of his uniqueness and small victories—moments of joy tucked between uncertainty—that have become some of my most cherished memories. Motherhood may be unpredictable, but mine has been filled with love, gratitude, growth, and resilience. And I wouldn't trade it for anything.

I never imagined I'd witness my baby boy suffer a sixteen-minute seizure following his vaccinations. That moment, one I wished I could unsee is seared into my memory—an image of helplessness, fear, shock, and disbelief. It sent ripples through my entire being, changing the way I approached everything related to his health.

In the aftermath, I learned the importance of doing my own research. I now take time to carefully consider every recommendation—especially when it concerns his body. We've chosen to move at his pace, allowing what's necessary and stepping away from rigid schedules or outside pressures. It's a decision rooted in trust—both in him and in my intuition.

Watching his natural abilities fade was devastating. His struggles with communication and social connection broke my heart. I could feel his frustration, even when he couldn't name it himself. This journey forced me to learn how to meet him where he was. But within that pain, I also witnessed extraordinary moments of triumph—glimpses of joy when he made progress, however small. Those wins replaced my sorrow with deep pride and gratitude.

In the beginning, I was fixated on all the hours of therapy he needed just to master skills that seemed to come so easily to others. My focus was narrow—I was chasing milestones and outcomes. But over time, I began to see something far more powerful: his ability to teach through connection. Every interaction with him became a lesson in empathy, understanding, and learning to slow down to see the world through his eyes.

His meltdowns used to leave me overwhelmed, unsure how to help. I mistook them for disobedience and attention seeking. But I've come to realize that these outbursts were his way of expressing emotions he couldn't yet put into words. That shift in perspective changed everything. Instead of reacting with frustration, I responded with patience and a soft tone—offering comfort when he needed it most.

I've also learned that he needs time to process before he speaks. Pressuring him to talk before he's ready only heightens his anxiety. At first, I didn't understand his silence or why he didn't respond or react as quickly as others do. But I now know he benefits from a gentle approach—step-by-step guidance, visual cues, and space. Adjusting my communication style has helped us create more open, trusting conversations.

Nothing prepared me for the day I found out he was being bullied. The anger and helplessness I felt at that moment still echo in my heart. It was crushing to see him mistreated—to know that his tenderness had been met with cruelty. I was filled with rage, wishing for a genie in a bottle to grant me a single wish. But even then, he showed me just how strong he is. His quiet resilience emerged, steady and unshaken, even in the face of deep pain.

While I might have responded differently, my son's reaction reminded me of the values we all strive to live by. His ability to remain compassionate—even toward those who have hurt him—reflects his strength of character and has taught me profound lessons in empathy and grace. Observing these qualities in Landon continues to inspire me, reminding me of the kindness that still exists in the world.

His compassion extends not just to people, but to animals and the environment as well. He carries a quiet graciousness that makes me long for a world with more people like him.

When Landon was very young, he was afraid of dogs. Then one day, he came home from preschool and asked for a puppy. His dad and I moved quickly, wanting to

support his curiosity before it faded. We discussed names and decided on a girl—we would call Hazel. Although he wasn't entirely sure about the name at first, that changed when we visited a litter of puppies. As we sat on the floor, one playful pup wouldn't stop licking him. He looked up at me and said, *"Look, Mommy, it's Hazel."* My heart melted—we had found our first dog.

A few years later, we welcomed Jax into our family. Landon loved being around dogs, and we felt Hazel deserved a companion. The two of them brought joy into our home, and it wasn't unusual to find all three of them—Landon, Hazel, and Jax—together in his room.

Having pets taught Landon responsibility, empathy, and unconditional love.

He also experienced the heartbreak of losing a beloved companion. Hazel passed away in June 2024, with all of us by her side. Though the pain still lingers, Landon came to understand something beautiful—that she was no longer suffering, and that love doesn't disappear with loss.

Early on, I admit I underestimated Landon's capabilities. But over time, his brilliance became undeniable. One of his most remarkable traits is his long-term memory. He recalls everything—from small details of our daily routines to appointments and household tasks. His mind keeps track in ways that often surprise me.

Even more incredible is how he brings memories to life. He can recall family vacations in exact order, describing

them like he's flipping through a mental scrapbook. When I forget things, he gently reminds me, filling in the blanks. His memory not only reflects his intellect—it strengthens our bond, keeping those shared moments alive.

When we travel, he always seems to know if I've missed a turn. His sense of direction is matched only by his passion for specific subjects. When something grabs his interest, he dives deep and tunes out distractions. His ability to focus—whether on a school assignment, a board game, or a bowling match—is striking. He approaches every task with clarity, determination, and care.

His focus not only helps him succeed but encourages those around him to rise to the occasion. These qualities have shaped the way he moves through the world—and I know they'll guide him toward future success.

As a young child, Landon had a unique habit of quietly observing others complete everyday tasks. At the time, I didn't understand why he preferred watching over participating. Later, I realized this was how he learned—by absorbing information, watching closely, and processing it in his own time. His observations weren't passive; they were intentional. He learned by watching, then applied those lessons when he was ready.

One of Landon's most admirable traits is his unwavering honesty. You can count on him to tell the truth in any situation. What makes it even more remarkable is how he does it with—politeness, tact, and respect. He knows how to share his thoughts without being hurtful, creating a space of openness and trust. His integrity is a cornerstone of his character and inspires others to value honesty in their own lives.

Another quality that stands out is his commitment to following rules. No matter where he is or who he's with, he adheres to every guideline. I sometimes joke that I'm glad I've always been law-abiding—otherwise, his honesty might get me in trouble! (Ha!) He truly believes in maintaining structure and won't make changes without permission.

I cannot fully express how heartbreaking it was to receive a diagnosis that could profoundly affect my son's development. In those early years, fear and uncertainty controlled my every action, word, and thought. However, over time, I realized that my feelings were natural, and taking swift action was not just helpful—it was essential. That sense of urgency became the foundation for his growth and helped shape him into the remarkable person he is today.

I wasn't prepared for the road ahead, and didn't realize my strength to navigate it. Later on, I realized I faced the moments before and after his diagnosis with optimism, determination, and resilience. I had to navigate this journey one day at a time. My focus became singular: to love him with everything I had and support him in every way I could.

Looking back, I realized no amount of preparation could have truly equipped me for what lay ahead.

Worry had become a persistent presence, haunting my every thought. But then came hope—a quiet but powerful shift. My love for him never wavered, but hope lit a fire within me. It pushed me to learn more, adapt, and work harder than I ever thought possible. That same hope inspired him, too. Together, we began moving forward, embracing everything, good and bad, with a plan and optimism.

Had I chosen denial instead of action, I believe my son's growth would have been stifled. I constantly ruminated on the what-ifs: What if I had listened to the doctor? What if I were too proud to accept our reality? What if I stopped fighting? I didn't realize then that his greatest tools were already within him—his strengths, his spirit, and his will to overcome. I also recognize that while denial crept in and tried to take hold, my body ultimately rejected it.

When I reflect on this journey, I realize the sacrifices—missed plans, sleepless nights, continuous learning, and emotional exhaustion—were all part of something much greater. Every moment of doubt, every breakthrough, and every struggle drew us closer.

Advocating for him requires not just unconditional love, but also patience, resilience, and a willingness to keep learning. While this path can be demanding, it becomes more manageable when I focus on his abilities. By building on his strengths, he will continue to grow in the areas that challenge him most.

This strength-based approach nurtures him and provides tools that will benefit him now and into adulthood. My goal is to help him become his own advocate, capable of facing life with clarity and courage. The thought of his voice rising above mine fills me with excitement. I eagerly await the moment when I can quietly watch him shine, allowing his charisma and brilliance to lead the way. I'm excited to see him take charge and share his important messages; I know he will inspire others with his unique insights.

My son inspires me daily. He continues to grow in ways that challenge and expand my understanding of who he is. I've come to see that he carries a rich world within him— full of thoughts, feelings, and insights waiting to be heard and appreciated. When I pause and truly listen, I'm struck by the depth of his wisdom.

Watching him embrace his life is a deeply humbling experience. It forces me to confront my own anxieties and limitations. And with every step he takes, my confidence grows too. His smallest victories ripple outward, reminding me that he's not just managing—he's thriving.

His perseverance and courage make him the bravest person I know. Each day, he teaches me what resilience truly means. This young man is not only my son—he is my greatest source of pride and gratitude. I am endlessly thankful for the person he's becoming and for the privilege of witnessing his growth. With each new day, I look forward to seeing the life he builds.

More than anything, seeing the world through his eyes has taught me to look deeper. His way of engaging with life— quietly observant, deeply curious—reveals beauty in places I once overlooked. His interpretations of the world challenge my assumptions, expand my thinking, and change how I move through the world—not just as a mother, but as a woman.

There is something extraordinary about how he approaches life with optimism and grace. He finds light in the shadows, discovers meaning in challenges, and consistently sees the good where others might not. Every moment with him is an opportunity to learn, grow, and share this beautiful journey—one filled with discovery, humility, and boundless love.

I am profoundly grateful for the many blessings that have unfolded throughout this journey. Above all, I treasure the extraordinary gift that God has given me—my son. Without ever speaking a word, he has taught me the deepest lessons in love and resilience as we faced challenges and found joy in life's simplest moments.

He illuminated the path for me to follow my instincts, guiding every decision and every step forward. This experience has helped me embrace the complexity and beauty of raising a child with autism, bringing us closer together and making us stronger in ways I never expected.

CHAPTER *13*

Milestones of Growth

Marking Progress on the Road Ahead

Landon is an inspiring young man who works hard every day to set and achieve his goals. He's loving, generous, patient, meticulous, thoughtful, and respectful. And his sense of humor? It lights up every room he walks into. Landon isn't just a remarkable person—he's also a focused bowler, a talented artist, and someone who always lends a hand without expecting anything in return.

When his emotions run high—whether he's excited, upset, or anxious—he sometimes babbles, engages in stim behaviors, or, at times, withdraws completely. While he has unique interests and is sensitive to certain stimuli, he also brings so many incredible qualities to the people around him.

He welcomes each day with gratitude, placing consistent care into both his physical and mental health through conversations, exercise, and mindful eating.

In the summer of 2023, Landon took the initiative to intern at a local fitness club, where he gained hands-on experience in health and wellness and learned the daily workings of the fitness industry. Outside of his internship, he contributes at home—tackling chores with a positive spirit, running errands with me, and keeping his priorities organized and in line with his goals.

Academically, Landon thrives. He's a high honor roll student, driven by dedication and self-discipline. In February 2025, he celebrated a major milestone—receiving the Student Achievement Award in Food Services II at his vocational school.

He puts genuine effort into all his classes and isn't afraid to ask for help when he needs it, which speaks to his perseverance and growth mindset. Math is his favorite subject, where his talent for numbers and problem-solving really shines.

Landon dreams of becoming a chef—fueled by his love of food and the happiness it brings to others. He believes that food has a special way of connecting people and creating memories, and that belief drives his passion for the culinary arts. He's excited to share his creativity through cooking and build a future where his food brings people together.

Landon's dream is to one day open a restaurant that welcomes everyone—including those with food allergies. His dedication to creating an inclusive dining experience is clear, rooted in his belief that everyone deserves to enjoy a meal together. That dream moved one step closer to reality when he received his acceptance letter into the culinary program at a local community college, where he begins classes in September 2025.

Although culinary arts remain Landon's passion, he spent a day as a student at the community college he plans to attend. Since culinary wasn't available that day, he chose the nursing program instead. His goal was to experience the college environment firsthand. When the program concluded and parents joined the information session, Landon surprised me by expressing genuine interest in nursing and a desire to explore it further.

It was unexpected to see him consider nursing as a backup, especially since becoming a chef has always been his dream. But I admired his insight. He spoke about the care he's received from doctors and nurses and how that inspired him to give back—to be a source of comfort and support for others facing similar challenges.

Landon also spent time reflecting on his artistic pursuits, revealing a deep passion for art that fuels his interest in animation. This creative path allows him to combine his love of storytelling with visual expression. While he doesn't see art as a career, he's committed to improving his skills and pursuing it as a lifelong hobby.

Bowling has transformed Landon's perception of himself both athletically and personally. Since he started bowling, he has committed himself to learning everything he can about it. He is receptive to advice, constructive criticism, and any changes that could improve his game. Bowling is not just a pastime he picked up in high school; it's a sport he aims to pursue as far as possible, with the goal of playing professionally one day.

With such wide-ranging interests and unwavering determination, Landon demonstrates exceptional character and limitless potential. I'm so proud of everything he's achieved and becoming.

He understands that not everyone will see the world the way he does—and that's okay. He knows his opinions may differ from others,' and he's learning to accept his strengths and his weaknesses as equally important parts of who he is. Landon has faced many challenges, some he's aware of and others he's only come to understand in time. I've walked alongside him through each one, reminding him that his resilience is exactly why I see him as the strongest person I know.

This is just a glimpse of what makes my son so perfect and unique—and I wouldn't change a single thing about him.

Every experience—his successes and struggles have helped shape who he is. As his mother, I've always encouraged him to be authentic and to embrace his potential, and I know he carries that encouragement with him.

Over the years, Landon has learned that his choices should reflect his values and goals, not someone else's expectations. He now understands that there's no single "right" path. His pursuit of perfection has shifted into a healthier pursuit of excellence—one that brings meaning rather than pressure. I've taught him that mistakes aren't failures; they're lessons. And growth, more often than not, comes from those very lessons.

Our connection runs deep. I see him, hear him, and understand him; I always have and always will. And I will always support his dreams with everything I have. His authenticity strengthens our bond, helping us navigate differences with kindness and mutual respect. Like him, I feel the full range of emotions and pursue my own dreams too. We simply do it in our own ways.

As he enters this next chapter of life, Landon holds the power to shape a meaningful future. Adulthood can be intimidating—full of change, uncertainty, and possibility—but I believe in his ability to handle it with courage. Together, we've started planning for this transition, using his strengths and passions to guide him. Step by step, we're preparing for what's ahead, knowing he's supported every inch of the way.

More than anything, I want to equip him with the knowledge, confidence, and tools he needs to build a life that feels right to him. Whether he's celebrating small victories or reaching major milestones, I'll be there—encouraging him, cheering him on, and reminding him just how far he's come.

As I reflect on our journey, I'm filled with gratitude—for the love we've shared, the support we've received, and the many moments that have left lasting imprints on our hearts. From his first day of school to blowing dandelions in the summer breeze, every memory has shaped who we are. Whether it was the splash of a puddle or the calm of a bedtime story, those simple moments taught us about joy, resilience, and the beauty of being present.

In our everyday lives, I've learned to treasure the small things: laughter over a meal, movie, or conversation, the warmth of a hug, the singing and dancing on a long car ride, and the comfort of shared silence. As Landon continues to grow and explore the world, I remain committed to creating a space where he feels safe, loved, and free to be and dream.

Being his mother has taught me more than I could have ever imagined. It's not just about learning who he is—

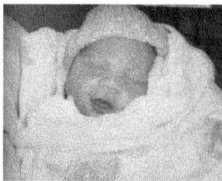

it's about discovering parts of myself I didn't know existed. I thank God every day for choosing me to be his mom and thank my son for the extraordinary gift of self-discovery he's given me in return.

Eighteen years ago, I welcomed him into this world—filled with wonder, unaware of the incredible person he would become. Looking back, I finally understand why I called him *"my little birdie."* It wasn't just a nickname I gave him when I saw him flap his hands; it was a gentle symbol of freedom, fragility, and possibility—a delicate soul ready to spread his wings.

Watching him grow has been a journey of a lifetime. From an innocent newborn to a curious toddler, and now to a young man with dreams, he has shown me what it means to love deeply and fiercely. He has also taught me the importance of perseverance. Every milestone, every smile, every word, and every moment has reaffirmed my promise to protect his joy, nurture his spirit, and support his flight—wherever it may take him.

A Letter to My Son

To my Prince,

Landon, my sweet boy, thank you for choosing me to be your mother. The day you were born will forever be the greatest day of my life. From the very first moment I learned of your existence, I loved you with a depth I hadn't known was possible and that love has only grown stronger as I've watched you become the remarkable person you are today. Every day, you remind me that simply being yourself is more than enough, and that authenticity continues to inspire me.

From the moment I felt your first flutter, I believed in you with all my heart and that belief has never wavered. My world revolves around your happiness, your growth, and your well-being. I would do anything—sacrifice, fight, move mountains, and face any challenge to ensure you have everything you need to thrive.

Every milestone you've reached fills me with immense pride, and I look forward to everything still to come. You carry within you—limitless potential. Whatever you dedicate your heart, your mind, and your spirit to—you can achieve. Always remember the strength that lives inside you; it will guide you through every challenge and triumph.

Autism may be a part of you, but it doesn't define who you are. You are everything I admire and aspire to be. You are special, and that is how God made you. Always embrace your individuality and remember how strong you are. Challenges may arise, but my commitment to turning those moments into something meaningful remains unshaken.

Each difficulty holds space for growth, and every obstacle offers a new lens—through which I see the brilliance within you. Together, we will navigate this life finding joy in the journey and power in the perspective you bring. Your spirit teaches me to see the world in brighter colors, and for that, I am forever grateful.

I've always admired the way you see the world—so vivid, so unique. In my world, you are the only thing I see, and it's breathtaking. You give my life meaning and purpose. You are my guiding star, lighting my way. And above all else, you are my heartbeat the steady rhythm that sustains my soul.

As you prepare to walk across not one but two stages in June 2025 to receive your high school diploma and culinary certificate, know how deeply proud I am of you. You earned it. This achievement is not only a celebration of your hard work and dedication but also a defining moment as you step into the next exciting chapter of your life. It speaks to your resilience and the incredible future that awaits you.

Life will test you in ways you never expected. When that happens, look within yourself first to find the strength to guide you, and reach out to others if you need help. Remember, asking for help is not a sign of weakness; it is one of the bravest things you can do and being brave is one of your strengths, trust me I know.

As you move through life, hold onto your kindness, curiosity and the spark that ignites your passions. If you ever find yourself drifting away from these qualities, take a moment to pause and immerse yourself in the beauty of the world around you and allow it to illuminate your path. Seek comfort in the simplest of things—the rain tapping the window, the birds flying in unison, the relaxation of a long car ride, or the smell of your favorite food. These small wonders can serve as a guiding light, leading you back to the essence of who you truly are and the joy you once knew.

Embrace the wings you've earned—built from determination and courage—and soar high toward your dreams. Trust your abilities. Let your passions guide you toward the life you dream of. The world is waiting to see the brilliance you have to offer, and I want you to always remember: my love for you stretches to the moon and beyond, an endless journey that knows no bounds.

I believe in you completely. I will always stand by your side, cheering you on as you reach for your dreams. You are extraordinary. Those who come into your life will see the incredible person that I see in you. You've shaped who I am, and that will never change. You are my everything—my baby boy, my Little Birdie. I love you to the moon and back and I will never, ever stop.

With all my love,

Mom

About the Author

Erica Taylor is a proud native of New Jersey. She is a mother, advocate, and dedicated professional. With a bachelor's degree in accounting, she began her career at the age of 17, driven by her passion for numbers and problem-solving. Erica enjoys long walks, listening to podcasts, cooking, journaling, and writing poetry. Above all, she loves spending time with her son, teaching him, and watching him succeed.

As an author, Erica self-published interactive journals for parents in 2019, designed to strengthen emotional bonds with their children. Her notable works include *Tell Me, Mom! Tell Me, Son!* and *Mom's Advice: Letters to My Son*, both crafted as a lasting legacy for her son. Through her writing, Erica aims to inspire meaningful conversations and create lasting memories for families.

A devoted mother, Erica faced the complexities of developmental challenges when her son was diagnosed with autism at just 26 months old. Since then, she has navigated every twist and turn of the journey with resilience, hope, and unwavering determination. Her advocacy is fierce and wholehearted, driven by a strong belief in her son's potential. She is constantly pursuing opportunities that support his growth and dreams.

Over the past 18 years, Erica has chronicled her and Landon's shared experiences, always knowing that the day would come when she would write a memoir and publish it after receiving her son's blessing.

With a deep understanding of the crucial conversations surrounding autism today, Erica hopes to offer encouragement, insight, and solidarity to others navigating similar paths. An autism diagnosis can be overwhelming, but she aims to help others see the beauty within it.

Her debut nonfiction book, *My Little Birdie to a Diagnosis*, is the first step in her mission to inspire and uplift families in the special needs community and to bring awareness and understanding to others. Believing that Landon's story reflects strength, empowerment, and unwavering hope, Erica is committed to showing others that they are not alone, and this book is only the beginning.

Additional Books

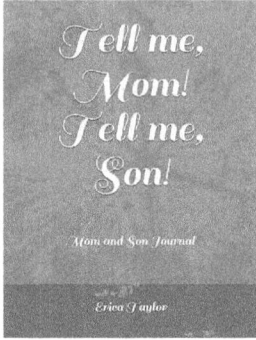

Tell me, Mom! Tell me, Son! — Mom and Son Journal — Erica Taylor

MOM'S ADVICE — LETTERS TO MY DAUGHTER

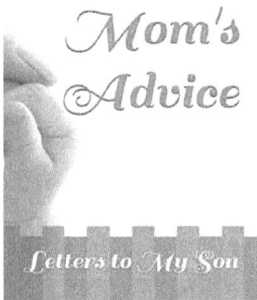

Mom's Advice — Letters to My Son

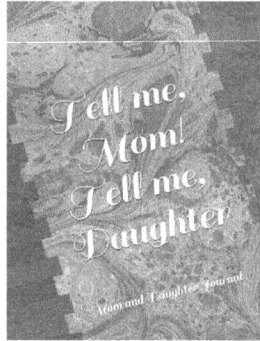

Tell me, Mom! Tell me, Daughter — Mom and Daughter Journal

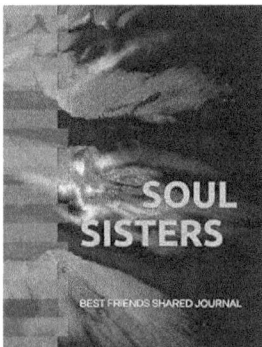

SOUL SISTERS — BEST FRIENDS SHARED JOURNAL

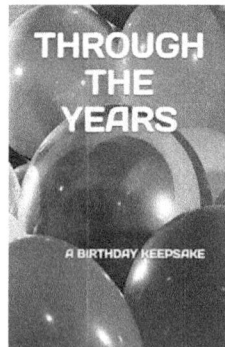

THROUGH THE YEARS — A BIRTHDAY KEEPSAKE

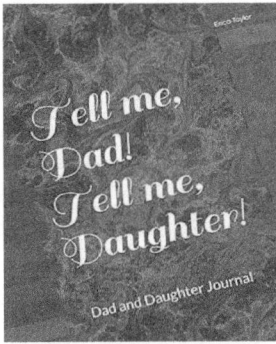

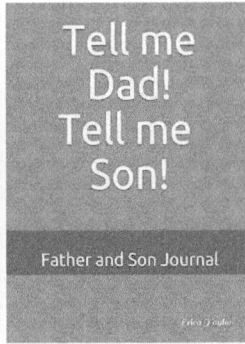

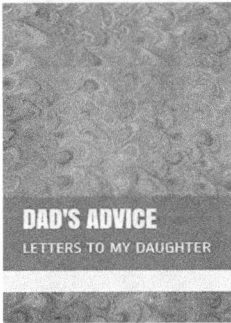

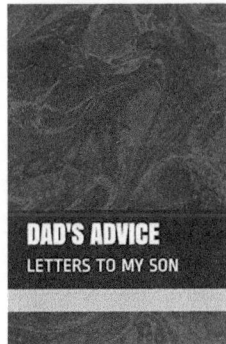

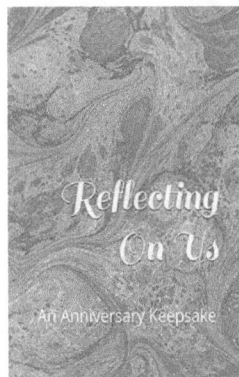

Find them on Amazon!

https://www.amazon.com/stores/author/B07RBBBTST

www.ingramcontent.com/pod-product-compliance
Lightning Source LLC
LaVergne TN
LVHW051110080426
835510LV00018B/1981